BUILDING THE
THERAPEUTIC SANCTUARY

The Fundamentals of Psychotherapy

From a Pastoral Counseling Perspective

BUILDING THE

THERAPEUTIC SANCTUARY

The Fundamentals of Psychotherapy

From a Pastoral Counseling Perspective

by Ron McDonald, D.Min.

Pastoral Counselor

Diplomate

American Association of Pastoral Counselors

authorHOUSE®

AuthorHouse™
1663 Liberty Drive
Bloomington, IN 47403
www.authorhouse.com
Phone: 1-800-839-8640

Published by AuthorHouse   09/11/2012

ISBN: 978-1-5882-0233-8 (sc)

TABLE OF CONTENTS

PREFACE

The purpose of this book is two-fold. First, I want to challenge the notion that a good therapist is mainly concerned with diagnosis and treatment plan. It is about relationship building, and the real care of a therapist is in the building of a sanctuary where a healing relationship can be nurtured. My problem is not with the process of diagnosis and treatment planning, it is in the idea that that is the most important part of the therapist's work. It is not. A layperson who can build and nurture a healing relationship well is a better therapist than an expert in diagnosis and treatment planning who short-changes relationship building.

Healing occurs at its deepest level in relationships. We are a relationship animal. We are not machines that can be made significantly better with technical expertise. The therapist's main task is to establish an authentic relationship and nurture it into life.

The second purpose of this book is to show the unique place of pastoral counseling in the mental health profession. Pastoral counselors, particularly those affiliated with the American Association of Pastoral Counselors, are not only some of the best trained psychotherapists in the field, but because of their theological training and years of working on the boundary between religion and psychology, are the best available interpreters of psychotherapy that takes religion seriously and uses it ethically in the therapeutic process.

Pastoral counseling's starting point for relationship-healing therapy is humility and faith. Humility is rooted in the Latin words *humilis*, which means low, small, or slight, and *humus*, which means soil or earth. The humble therapist is one who knows he or she is of the earth, not the heavens. Even great training experiences do not make the humble therapist act bigger than he or she is. And faith, I shall explain carefully in this book, is not the same thing as belief. Beliefs close doors. Beliefs are security blankets that we all have and need. Faith, however, means openness—radical, undefended openness. Faith is the touchstone of relationship-healing therapy.

The paradox of this book is that I am presenting a principled, somewhat strict blue-print for building the therapeutic sanctuary while suggesting that one begins therapy with humility and faith. I want the therapist to carefully attend to many details in the sanctuary building process, then let go of them and be genuine, humble, and open.

It is like what happens to the athlete. In order to become good at a sport, the athlete must break it down into small muscle movements and train repetitively until those movements are fluid and easy, then, at the point of competition, perform them with hardly a thought about them. Just as the best athletic performance comes on the heels of intense training but looks relaxed and easy, the therapist must take great care of every detail of the sanctuary he or she is building, then relax and be open.

Finally, I should say what this book is not. It is not an academic treatise. I draw on theory and scholarly work, but I do not pretend to be a scholar. I am first and foremost a practical clinician, and this book is a description of a clinician's method of creating a therapeutic sanctuary. I seek to present a theoretical framework that has integrity, but I doubt that it would stand up to an academic test. I seek to stay consistent with a working theory, but I have to plead with Emerson, "I'm inconsistent; so, I'm inconsistent." What I'm trying to do instead is to help one think systematically about the creation of a place where good therapy can take place.

I hope that this book helps therapists build relationship-healing sanctuaries, and then encourages them to relax and "love the one you're with."

INTRODUCTION

Psychotherapy in this age of managed care and time-limited patient contact is in danger of losing its most important discipline: the discipline of creating a sound, safe, and healing relationship. Most of the training psychotherapists receive today is in how to become a technician. We have learned how to be technically helpful, often at the expense of personableness. With the burgeoning focus on diagnosis and treatment plan has come an efficiency in helping people that is often incompatible with the essence of good relationships, and if, as is my assertion, the most significant healing occurs in the relationship between therapist and client, then psychotherapy as it is being most commonly practiced is often trivial in the healing process. The trouble is that we are teaching therapists that the correct beginning place for psychotherapy is diagnosis and treatment plan. That is a mistake. The place to begin is in the relationship, and the way to do that is to begin with building a solid frame, a sanctuary for healing.

Students and supervisees of mine have typically been most responsive to descriptions of how to specifically do psychotherapy. The way I teach psychotherapy is to avoid the focus on technique so prevalent today, and instead seek to describe the tedious care that must be taken in the creation of the therapeutic sanctuary. That sanctuary is what has been commonly referred to as the frame of therapy. I use these terms interchangeably. They both evoke a sense of boundary, although the word "sanctuary" also evokes the sacred, which is what the best relationships evoke. Martin Buber used the terms "I-it" and "I-Thou" to contrast relationships that are objectified and cold with those that are respectful and warm. I see therapists being trained in

xi

I-it styles of relating in order to protect their professional status and over-involvement with clients. One purpose of this book is to present a way of treating clients in an I-Thou manner, creating a truly care-full sanctuary.

When I was a beginning psychotherapist, the best book I read on psychotherapy was Sheldon Kopp's *Back to One*, a primer on the details of the psychotherapeutic frame. Over the years I have recommended *Back to One* more than any other book as a basis for psychotherapy. The intent of this book is not to replace but to compliment Kopp's book. I have my own way of creating a good therapeutic frame. Although it is very similar to Kopp's, what I have to say adds a theological base for understanding relationships. This book expands on Kopp's work by tapping much of what I have learned as a pastoral counselor. What makes pastoral counseling unique among the psychotherapy disciplines is its rich insights into the interplay between theology and psychology. Theology is about asking universal questions of meaning, and psychology is about asking individual questions of meaning. Having some theological sophistication adds clarity to the psychotherapy discipline that has made an enormous difference in my work. I think it will be helpful to the apprentice therapist, seasoned therapist, as well as the master therapist.

This book is founded upon a simple theory: relationships are what heal, and they are best fostered by reverently treating the emotional, spiritual, and physical space around clients—creating a sanctuary. Most of what I write about is the practical, detailed application of this theory. The central theory will be referred to and clarified throughout the book, although my thinking is practical and clinical and does not suffice as an academic, theoretical treatise.

The book is divided into three parts. *Part One* is about setting up a psychotherapeutic environment and creating the frame of therapy. *Part Two* is about interacting with a new client in a way that creates a relationship sanctuary where healing can take place. *Part Three* is a description of therapeutic phases of change through a successful long-term psychotherapy experience.

It is my hope that this book will serve to give the reader an idea about how to be care-full in the development of a relationship. Good relationships can happen naturally in time, but therapists often don't have the luxury of six months of treatment in order to let a good relationship evolve like therapists used to in the days of psychoanalytical treatment. Nowadays we have to speed up the relationship building process, and the way this is normally done in the field is to make a diagnosis and create a treatment plan. We seem to think that focusing more on the patient will make psychotherapy more efficient. That is a mistake. This book is an attempt to correct that mistake by helping us focus instead on the relationship. If we spend our careful energy on the beginnings of a relationship instead of on the patient, we will quickly tap into the most powerful healing element in the therapeutic process.

PART ONE
THE BUILDING BLOCKS OF A
SANCTUARY FOR HEALING

CHAPTER ONE
THE THERAPIST

Somewhere along the vocational way, a person will feel a call or urge to become a psychotherapist. For many doctors it happened when they discovered meaning in their psychiatry rotations while in medical school. Many clinicians began from a personal experience in therapy, finding themselves fascinated with the therapeutic process and wanting to help others as they were helped. Many were fascinated with psychology and wanted to work in the setting where psychology is applied. Many found themselves in a role that required counseling skills to help those who sought their help. They decided to advance their skills from counselor to psychotherapist. Many entered the profession because they needed help themselves and found it to be scratching a particular itch. There is no right or wrong reason for seeking to become a therapist. The learning process itself is designed to weed out the neurotic needs from the health-enhancing ones. The route to becoming a therapist usually transforms the budding therapist from idealist or neurotic to realistic clinician.

Currently there are five routes to becoming a therapist. These routes vary somewhat from state to state, but not significantly. You may become a psychiatric social worker, a psychologist, a psychiatrist, a marriage and family therapist, or a pastoral counselor. Psychiatric social workers must receive a Masters degree in Social Work, usually a two year program, and then go through an extensive state licensing program and examination, which usually takes another three years of closely supervised work. A psychologist must earn a Ph.D. in clinical psychology, usually 5 years of graduate academic and clinical work, then take a clinical licensing examination. A psychiatrist must earn a four year Doctor of Medicine degree, work under close supervision in internships and residencies for 4 more years, and pass a medical board examination. A marriage and family therapist must earn a Masters in Counseling that includes specific coursework, usually two years of graduate work, and complete a structured supervisory period of clinical work that usually takes two more years, and pass an examination. A pastoral counselor must earn a Master of Divinity degree (which takes three years), receive a Masters in Counseling or certification from a clinical training program (usually two years' training), be closely supervised for another one to three years, then pass a careful committee examination. Regardless of the route one takes, becoming a psychotherapist is a long haul. And, the truth is that one is rarely a good psychotherapist without seven or more years of clinical experience under one's belt. Under the close supervision an apprentice therapist receives, the quality of therapy is usually kept quite high, particularly when one is part of the various therapeutic guilds like the American Association of Marriage and Family Therapists, the American Association of Pastoral Counselors, the American Medical Association, etc. Those therapists who do not belong to the various professional guilds are not necessarily poor therapists, but they do not have a collective group overseeing the quality of their work.

The beginning psychotherapist should first look into the requirements of the guild he or she is interested in. Basically, guilds will require four things: (1) a sound theoretical foundation that the therapist can thoroughly articulate, (2) substantial clinical guidance from approved supervisors, (3) an extensive amount of clinical experience, and (4) personal integrity and insight.

Theoretical Foundation

Any training program has to be grounded in a clear, understandable, practical theoretical point of view. Most programs seek to teach one particular theoretical point of view. There should be room for divergent theories, but there is much wisdom in the idea that learning one perspective well provides a litmus test for validating and applying any other theory. In other words, if you know one theory well, you have the basis for intelligent dialog with other theories or theorists.

I was a competitive runner in college and afterwards. I studied running in great depth, getting to know the fundamentals of form, training methods, and competitive strategies very well. When I became a coach of other sports later, I found that the understanding of that one sport gave me the foundation for understanding the fundamentals of the others. Even though much of the skills were different, the training and methods of application were parallel. Because I knew one sport well, I could understand others quickly and recognize the limits of my knowledge. The same is true for understanding the various schools of psychology. Learning one in depth gives one the ability to understand others quickly and apply their insights properly.

Training programs do well to teach one theory well, but I have noticed that many such programs and teachers become "fundamentalists" in that theory to the critical exclusion of other theories. They subscribe to their theory with hardly a trace of humility and openness to the validity of others. Thus, they tend to train technicians who apply their theories to their clients in a rather disengaged manner, not acknowledging the need for fresh perspectives in some difficult cases.

Good training depends on a balance between the teaching of a sound theoretical base and the humility to know that that theory is just one of many good ones. This gives the student the freedom to find or develop a theory that is not only professionally helpful, but personally satisfying. The purpose of learning one theory well is to train the mind, not to create instructions on how to do psychological surgery.

My Theoretical Foundation

Although I still recommend my supervisees read psychodynamic theorists, Jungian literature, and Bowenian theory, my own theoretical foundation is now more along the lines of a theology of nonviolence. Although is it is beyond the scope of this book to elucidate that theory, much of its application will be evident here. Let me simply present my starting point.

A Northern Senator after the Civil War challenged Abraham Lincoln to thoroughly punish the defeated Southerners. The Senator said, "I was taught early on to utterly destroy my enemies," to which Lincoln testily replied, "Sir, it is clear to me that if we befriend our enemies, we do destroy them."

That is my starting point as a therapist. If someone comes to me having anxiety attacks, I begin from the position that the anxiety attacks, debilitating as they presently are, need to be befriended. The reason behind the attacks is often crucial to the client's quest for wisdom.

Wisdom is a combination of two things: (1) the inner sense of knowing and being known, and (2) insight into the nature of life. This is where theology meets psychology. Theologically, the sense of knowing and being known is a leap of faith. I have often asked clients who are experiencing transformational health, "How do you know you are ok?"

6

They never really have a straight-forward answer. Instead, they reply in paradox, "I don't know, but I do know." Our knowledge of what the good life is about, and for that matter, what bad life is about, is more than a philosophical position or even a common sense position. It is a faith position, a sense of knowing which words cannot approach. The same is true with being known. When we are truly touched at the depths of our being, as the psychoanalyst Heinz Kohut would say, something primordial resonates within, giving us knowledge of touch and caring that is beyond words or explanation. Such touch is deeply healing.

Psychology is the knowledge of the soul (psyche = soul; ology = wisdom or knowledge). The foundation for all psychology is the parallel experiences of touching and being touched. As simple as it sounds, good therapy is like a good handshake. One cannot tell who is giving and who is receiving. A handshake with someone who does not return the firmness of the grip is not a meaningful handshake, just as is a handshake with someone who crushes your hand. To be able to give and receive a handshake properly is the metaphor I use to understand the deepest level of psychological importance in the therapeutic process.

A piano player once came to see me, and upon introducing ourselves we shook hands. With a friendly smile on his face, speaking warmly towards me, he almost broke my hand. Surprisingly, at the end of the session, when he offered me his hand again, and I returned mine—carefully this time and fully ready to fight off his strength—he gave me a soft, lifeless, weak handshake. Obviously, something had happened in the session that he had very little consciousness of. He needed help with that. The psychological purpose of therapy is to help the client develop a clear and more accurate sense of self, to help one become more conscious, and less unconscious, of who one is. It is also to help one encounter the depth of the unconscious self so that one can respect it, befriend it, and listen to its images and messages.

One's wisdom is incomplete without a healthy level of insight into one's family of origin. The experiences of one's childhood family are so tremendously powerful that they are the key to how one gets along in any system and the level of individuation one can achieve. Most simply, the work of therapy must include helping one look with objectivity at one's family of origin for the purpose of developing a level of differentiation that liberates from the coercive forces any family develops.

For me the questions I ask about a therapist's theoretical orientation are these three:

(1) Does it begin from wisdom gleaned from suffering, helping the client respect a transcendent dimension of healing?

(2) Does it help the client seek answers from the inner life, respecting and befriending the unconscious self?

(3) Does it help the client make sense of childhood and family of origin influence on one's present-day life, allowing one to choose one's own path?

My theoretical foundation can be summed up as a combination of theology, psychoanalytic theory, and family systems theory. I start from the theological position that there is a transcendent dimension in all relationships that will affect open and honest relationships in a healing way. I take it as a given that wounds are the basis for wisdom, and that one's joy in life is equal to the depth of pain one has experienced. Stated mythologically, there is no resurrection without a cross, no deliverance without bondage, no Promised Land without traveling through a desert. Thus,

8

I begin with the hope and confidence that the pain and suffering my clients bring to therapy are the beginning of their own liberation. What we are therefore seeking is the blessing inherent in the curse. In short, I believe that all of life is a gift waiting to be received. Suffering is certainly not the gift, but the wisdom God might grant us is packaged in the suffering and relief in this life.

CHAPTER TWO
CLINICAL SUPPORT

No one becomes a therapist just by studying psychology, just as no one becomes a doctor by just studying science or a minister by just studying theology. The bridge between academic discipline and practical skill is mentoring. It is a relationship with a teacher, or more accurately, a series of teachers.

Supervision of one's work will be the foundation of one's clinical skills. It should take three directions:

1) work with a guild-approved supervisor one-on-one;
2) work with a variety of clinicians from a variety of orientations in a disposition or diagnostic conference; and
3) work on one case with a small group of colleagues and a supervisor for an extended period of time.

Individual Supervision

It is not possible to become a good therapist without sitting many hours one-on-one with a supervisor. Such a consultant provides knowledge of how to apply theory, how to make it practical, how to use words and phrases effectively, oversight of one's working style and structure, a model, and support through confusing and anxious times. Becoming a therapist is a very intensive and difficult task, and the individual supervisor is probably the most important person in the beginning phase of work. To have someone to help the beginning therapist find strengths and challenge weaknesses in a non-critical, helpful way is impossible to do without. The good supervisor will become a mentor.

One does not choose a mentor, but one does choose persons likely to become mentors. Thus, it is important to carefully choose a supervisor. Most training programs offer supervision as part of their tuition, which means that the supervisor will be chosen for the beginning therapist. That usually works well early in one's work, but as one progresses it is advisable to consider paying for and contracting the supervisor of one's choice—one that is approved by the training program one is part of.

When I began training I had a supervisor who was willing to barter for his services. Since I had little money, that sounded great. For a while the relationship worked well, for I was mainly just getting my feet wet and sharing my fascination with the confessional nature of the work. I had spent over three years myself in life-changing, psychodynamic-oriented psychotherapy and felt quite sure of the validity of that approach to doing therapy. My supervisor, however, was primarily a behaviorist who scorned long-term therapy. He thought I had wasted my money. Soon we began to conflict, and since I was newer at the work than he was, I was thrown into much confusion. Eventually my confusion became anger, for as I grew in my ability I saw his perspectives as judgmental and discounting of the healing quality of a long-term relationship. At that point I realized that continuing supervision with him was going to be troublesome. I quit with him and carefully chose another supervisor, tightening my belt and paying a real fee.

I'm not advocating seeking a supervisor who will not challenge your work, for my subsequent supervisors have always challenged me greatly. I'm simply advocating choosing a supervisor with whom you are compatible, particularly one whose theoretical foundation is compatible with what you are seeking. My first supervisor's working theory was incompatible with my experience and training orientation.

Interdisciplinary Case Conference

Interdisciplinary Case Conference is normally a gathering of clinicians who assess and determine the best course of treatment for the presented clients. Usually included are a psychiatrist, a psychologist, a social worker, a family therapist, a person skilled at working with addictions, and often a pastoral counselor. Students participate as presenters and receive the experienced insight of all who wish to address the case. Write-ups are carefully prepared and presented to facilitate the process, and time schedules for analyzing the presentations are used to insure that the scheduled number of presentations are completed. Such conferences are excellent ways to get a feel for the variety of ways clinicians work and look at clients or patients, and they help the student realize how many views there are about how to properly treat problems. It is not an exact science. Disagreement is common and appropriate. In a good case conference, latitude is given to the student in consultation with his or her individual supervisor to determine how to treat the client.

Small Group Supervision

Often called "Group Soup" with 4-6 students and one supervisor, this is often the most enjoyable of all one's educational experience, for here is where the student learns the most from other students and becomes a colleague. Good teachers know that a crucial learning ingredient is intra-student dialog. Students learn tremendous amounts from one another when they develop good rapport, and they often continue to learn from one another throughout their entire careers.

This style of supervision works best when it is a "continuous case conference," which means that the group tracks one client of each student for an extended period of time, helping the beginning clinician understand the problems, issues, and clinical needs as the case unfolds.

CHAPTER THREE
COMMUNITY SUPPORT

The good therapist does not work alone. A therapist who seeks to be entirely independent is normally hiding major ethical misbehavior or narcissistic conflicts. It is the community of like-minded therapists who keep the individual therapist from wandering off into the pit-falls of the profession—places where one succumbs to the temptation to make guarantees for a particular technique, giving advice too freely, encouraging clients to be somewhat worshipful of the therapist's skill and wisdom, using clients for sex, and otherwise blurring the boundaries of good ethical behavior. A therapist working entirely alone is a threat to the larger therapeutic community. Every therapist needs to be active in a guild that oversees his or her work.

I am a member of the American Association of Pastoral Counselors. The purpose of the A.A.P.C. is "to promote the ministry of pastoral counseling and the professional competence of pastoral counselors" (AAPC, 1993). For me this organization has offered
1) a wonderful collegial network,
2) a blueprint for quality education and training,
3) continuing education,
4) a rigorous credentialing process,
5) some degree of legal protection,
6) community recognition, and
7) ethical clarification.

A.A.P.C. is one of the smaller of the professional counseling guilds, but its standards may be the highest. So I'll use it as a model for what a guild can be for the clinician.

In the A.A.P.C. there is a four-tiered credentialing process. First, one becomes a Pastoral Counselor in Training (P.C.T.) by presenting an educational plan to the regional certification committee. In return the trainee is assigned a mentor, a seasoned pastoral counselor, as a guide, friend, and developing colleague. Education for the trainee is expected to include training in the sub-discipline of theology, theoretical training in psychotherapy, clinical training, and personal therapy. Virtually all training in psychotherapy should contain these four areas of work, and all the guilds certainly require the first three, many the fourth—personal therapy. The reason why some guilds do not require personal therapy is because there is a large wing in psychology and psychotherapy that is treating therapy as a technical process. Technicians do not necessarily need personal therapy. They simply must learn the proper procedures and techniques and follow the rules. Relationship-oriented therapy that is seen as embracing the intuitive, the artistic, as well as the scientific will always need the therapists to be personally insightful and aware of oneself, and there is no better way to achieve a high level of personal insight at a young age than personal therapy.

For one to become a Member-Certified of A.A.P.C., the course of study one embarked upon as a P.C.T. will have to be completed, including passing a competency exam and a meeting with a committee for review.

In A.A.P.C. there are two more levels of membership which move one into position to be seen as a guild mentor. A Fellow is one who has achieved a second academic degree in psychotherapy, has a large amount of clinical experience while under supervision, and has demonstrated an ability to teach. He or she can therefore work independently and supervise beginning therapists while under supervision of their supervision. At this level the therapist must meet a Certification Committee for a rigorous face-to-face review, unless one is fully certified through another guild or state and only now becoming a member of A.A.P.C. This meeting is the crucial guild acceptance process. One must be able to demonstrate personal confidence, strength, insight, and sensitivity before one's colleagues. This process is at the heart of the strength of any guild, because any guild is by definition exclusive, and to be included through a hard-to-earn acceptance process genuinely initiates one into the guild community. The trouble with this process is that it can easily become a male initiation rite, in which the applicant is expected to stand up to the aggression of the committee members in order to prove his manhood. That process might not be bad for men to have to go through, but when an organization is multi-sexual and multi-cultural such initiation passages are inappropriate. Fortunately for the A.A.P.C. and other guilds, women and persons from other cultures are forcing the certification process to focus on competency, not manhood.

Diplomates are those who have had extensive supervisory experience and have demonstrated an understanding of the supervisory process, again including a face-to-face review. They can supervise supervisors.

Guild standards vary, but they are basically similar to these. Each guild typically claims that their standards are the most difficult to achieve and are often derisive of the "easy" standards of other guilds, but that's just community self-righteousness. The truth is that all guilds require a lot and it will continue to be an arduous process to become a psychotherapist, regardless of the route one takes to get there.

CHAPTER FOUR
PERSONAL HELP

The most important part of therapy for anyone is the development of a style or manner for dealing with suffering. Therapy is about healing, but since life is and always will be wounding, therapy will always be about helping the client develop ways to cope with emotional pain and systemic suffering.

Since suffering is the root of wisdom, it only follows that therapy, which can be seen as the intentional confrontation of the depth of suffering in one's life, is an encounter with wisdom. One could say that a therapist is a personification of the goddess of wisdom, Sophia.

It continues to amaze me that persons who seek my counsel often describe what helpful things I've said to them in ways that one might describe the wise King Solomon. Usually what they are referring to are obscure comments I made which I don't even remember saying. Of course I like to take the full credit for expounding such wisdom, but the truth is that the wisest things I happen to say come spontaneously, accidentally, and often without any awareness of the impact they might have on the client. What I understand to be happening is that I have unconsciously connected with their own wisdom archetype, the god/goddess-of-wisdom-within, so that they are able to turn my simple words into deep insights. They are essentially projecting god-like qualities onto me, mistaking me for their own inner wisdom, which therapy is helping them reconnect with. Jesus called this "throwing pearls to swine", that is, projecting our best onto someone who is not nearly as good or wise as we imagine them to be.

The power and exaltation that a therapist enjoys—and we do enjoy it!—can be intoxicating. Sometimes we therapists begin to believe in our own wisdom, our own healing power. We lose touch with the old aphorism that "I am not the healer, but only the instrument of God's healing power." It happens to me very often. A client will have a very healing and insight-filled session, and as he or she leaves, I burst out in pride and think, "I did a great job. I'm a Master Therapist." Then the next client comes in to be blessed by my amazing abilities, and, lo and behold, I begin to feel lost, and somewhere in the middle of the session the client will say, "I'm feeling more confused now than I did when I came in." My bubble bursts.

The self-righteous, conceited therapist is a lousy therapist!

The greatest antidote to such blasphemy ("I am like a god.") is personal therapy. To finally admit that I need help and insight, that I can't seem to autonomously solve all my problems, and to make that phone call to a mysterious therapist is a very humbling experience. It is very hard to do. I know it is, for I have made that call myself a number of times, and each time I feel as though I'm admitting defeat, admitting my own inability to cope with problems. But if I hadn't made those calls, I might very well ridicule those who complain that they didn't really want to come see me, that they feel like therapy should be unnecessary. I might say with an inward sneer, "Would you set your own broken bones?" Even though that question might help someone accept the need for therapy, asked from a self-righteous vantage point it might add wound to the wounds. The therapist must understand from personal experience the courage it takes to seek professional help, for the humble attitude of the therapist is the most important attitude he or she offers the client.

The most important reason why therapists need personal therapy is to develop humility. They might gain much wisdom and insight from the experience, but most importantly, they need great doses of humility to be a good therapist. Clients may think we're gods and goddesses, but we in fact have feet of clay. Healing happens in therapy often in spite of us, and it does most often when we remember to put on the mantle of humility. This mantle is always there as long as we remember our own difficulties and struggles. We therapists are not necessarily any healthier than those who seek our help.

What the good therapist has, though, that the client doesn't have, is not only specialized knowledge, but a broadened experience from having taken advantage of personal therapy. Good therapists have usually been in therapy much longer than their clients. I think that a therapist needs at least five years of therapy before he or she can deeply understand the therapeutic process. Individual supervision may be the most important process in the development of the professional skill of therapy, but personal therapy determines the degree of integrity and selfhood the therapist brings into the therapeutic process. There is no way around the need of therapists for years of personal therapy. We may want short-cuts, but there are none. To be a good therapist, one has to have been a client for some time.

Besides, therapists in training can gain the most from their personal therapists. Being disciplined students of the therapeutic process, trainees know how to use their therapist's help best. As a therapist I enjoy working with other therapists immensely. Of course, some have found ways to use their insights into the therapeutic process as great intellectual defenses, but generally they are excellent clients. And I know what they mean when they talk about how therapy is helping their work. When I'm in personal therapy, I'm typically at my best as a therapist. Not only am I better in touch with myself, but I'm experiencing a rich modeling process. The individual supervisor, model that he or she is, hardly rivals the modeling provided by the personal therapist, for when personal therapy is making a difference in one's life, we have intimate knowledge of what works well in therapy.

The best coach I ever had would never try to teach us an athletic skill without first seeking himself to become proficient at it. Even when he did not achieve proficiency, the fact that he had attempted to master the skill had taught him to respect the skill in a special way, and it made him a better teacher. The best thing a therapist can do for his or her clients is to be a client.

CHAPTER FIVE
STRUCTURE OF THE JOB

We now turn from functional concerns to structural concerns, that is from the personal and professional posture to practical matters. And first on the list of what the therapist needs is a sound employment structure. Fortunately, being a therapist does not require much. To some extent all that is required is a person seeking help and a therapist willing to listen. That can be done outdoors on a hike. But to be successful at the business, more conventional means invariably must be addressed. Here are the conventional needs.

Financial Clarity

There are essentially four ways in which therapists are paid: salary, commission, salary plus commission, and an administrative fee basis. Each of them has their strengths. On a salary basis the therapist will have to answer to a statistical accounting of his or her work. If one is paid to see 25 persons a week for a set salary, not doing that amount of work is grounds for reprimand or dismissal. Organizations that pay salaries do not work well if there are not a large number of clients being referred. If there aren't 25 clients available to see each week, the therapist will have to invent some creative ways to justify one's salary. In the long run, one can't. Salary systems also mean that the therapist is not directly motivated to charge the full fee. Organizations that pay salaries often have a lower average fee than others, for their therapists are not directly affected by fee adjustments.

A commission basis gives one more job security in exchange for taking responsibility for one's personal income. There is a high financial ceiling, but no floor.

That is, one can earn a lot of money, but if one is doing poorly, the organization suffers less than the therapist does. Most commission contracts are in the 60-75% range—the therapist receiving 60-75% of all fee revenues and the organization the smaller percentage. It is not uncommon for well-established therapists to be seeing 1400 client hours a year with a hefty average fee. On a purely commission basis (70%) these therapists are returning a great deal of their collections to the organization for administrative costs. Most therapist balk such costs unless the organization provides some major benefits in exchange.

One of the benefits often provided is an administrative salary, creating a salary plus commission basis. Such a contract provides for the therapist a financial floor plus a high ceiling. Under this system a therapist might be paid $1000 a month in salary for contracted administrative work and also receive 70% of fees collected. Under such systems the therapist is directly connected to fee revenue collections as well as firmly connected and committed to the organization. If the therapist's fee collections suffer, the organization also suffers. Many organizations which use this salary package receive some funding from outside sources to help absorb the salary they are responsible for paying.

An arrangement that is very common is that of each therapist paying a portion of the organization's administrative costs. This is essentially a rental agreement. Someone or an organization provides administrative services that are paid for by benefiting therapists. For example, an office might cost $2000 a month to rent and operate, and the organization might have four therapists. Each of them would contract to pay $500 a month to cover common expenses. Under such arrangements often if a therapist wants more administrative support services than the other therapists do, he or she will have to contract separately for them from an outside source. Therapists under these arrangements sometimes take care of their own billing and bookkeeping, and thus the organization has little financial control beyond the agreed upon office fee.

I have worked under all four arrangements and have found that none is innately better than another. All work well when caseloads and collections are strong. None of them work well when caseloads and collections are weak. Presently I am paid a set salary. I like it because it gives me a great deal of security. I don't like it because I don't feel particularly connected to the fees I generate, which are considerably lower than I used to collect. However, it allows me to work with more poor people, which I value. Prior to my present position I was on a salary plus commission basis. In it I had a great deal of security and loyalty to the organization, but since salaries were uneven in the organization, jealousy was present and not particularly healthy for us. There is no perfect system.

Fee Policy

There are essentially three fee policies: a set fee, an adjustable fee, and a sliding fee scale. When insurance coverage is involved the therapist must charge a set fee, and it must be the same for both the client and the insurance company. Some therapists have gotten into trouble by charging a cut rate fee to the client and the full fee to the insurance company. Insurance policy is a co-pay policy whereby the client must pay a set percentage of the fee after paying the entire deductible, and if the therapist and client have colluded to reduce the client's burden, while billing insurance companies the full amount, this is a breach of contract with the insurance company. In other words, if a therapist's fee is $100 an hour and the insurance company pays 50% after the deductible is reached, the client and the insurance company must both pay $50. If the therapist charges the client only $25 while sending the insurance company a bill for $100, the actual fee is being misrepresented to the insurance company. The actual fee is $75, for that is all the therapist is expecting to be paid. Such arrangements cheat the insurance company and are, in fact, illegal.

All therapists' fees are adjustable. Even when a therapist says flatly, "My fee is . . . .", he or she will be negotiable on certain days. Sometimes they meet a client who is particularly intriguing but cannot pay the flat fee. Sometimes they are worried about their caseload. Sometimes they are feeling generous. And sometimes, of course, their caseloads are full, they do not feel generous, and the client does not seem exceptional or intriguing enough, and the therapeutic fee is in fact non-negotiable. But I have never known a therapist with a totally non-negotiable fee structure.

Sliding fee scales based upon income are common with organizations that are community supported. They are also the organizations most often cheated by client misrepresentation. Most people have means of taking care of emergency financial needs, and sliding fee scales usually don't tap into those means. If a therapist looks at a sliding fee scale based upon the client's income and suggests a fee, if the fee is within the client's means, the client does not have to go to emergency resources. And sometimes those emergency resources are substantial. I once was charging a couple a mere $17 a session based upon a couple's income and the recommended fee of the organization I worked for, and after about 15 sessions, as we were ending the treatment, they thanked me for not forcing them to use any of their $42,000 in savings. All I could say was, "You're welcome," but I was furious at them, at myself, and at the sliding fee scale. Another time I negotiated a $30 a session fee with a young woman who intimated that that fee would be hard for her to pay, but she could do it. A number of sessions later I found out that her wealthy parents were paying the whole amount. Organizations that use sliding fee scales usually have a very low average fee. I think it's a poor system for middle class clients. A sliding fee scale should be used only as a guideline for thinking about what kind of fee won't turn people at certain income levels away from seeking counseling help. The fee should be negotiated based on other factors as well.

Office Requirements

There are two simple requirements for a therapist's office: a counseling room with chairs, lighting, and heat, and a waiting room with chairs, lighting, and heat. Some think air conditioning is necessary, too, but a fan will work. The counseling room must have walls and doors that do not allow sound transfer. There are two ways to accomplish this. One is to hang two doors, sound deaden the walls of the office, and cover up the crack under the door(s). Another is to place music or a sound box in the waiting room to interfere with the voices from the counseling room. The best way is to have good solid walls and doors and play music in the waiting room.

Beyond the minimal requirements, the client's second impression of the therapist is the office environment. An opulent office gives one impression; a threadbare one another. My preference is simplicity, partly out of my psychoanalytically-oriented training (purists suggest blank walls or landscape art), partly because I'm not an opulent person. My counseling office and waiting room is my work home, so I decorate it to my liking.

The telephone is an essential part of the therapist's work, one that needs some attention. Therapists typically use three means of answering the phone when they are in session or unavailable: voice mail, answering service, or receptionist. A good receptionist is invaluable. Calls, especially the first one, are rife with tension from the client, and a personal, businesslike receptionist goes miles towards drawing a client into the healing environment the therapist is seeking to develop. Answering services are, in my opinion, a mistake. I know many therapists who love them, but they almost always make me angry. They go between the actual office and the client, and I personally don't have a great deal of patience with middle-people when simply trying to leave a message. I'd rather talk to voice mail. Since there are almost always messages to return between sessions, having hourly access to a phone is essential. I've had difficult access to a phone in an office before, and it is not only annoying, but it hurts one's practice, for returning calls promptly is essential to a good impression.

Nowadays malpractice insurance is considered an essential part of one's practice. Mine costs $180 a year. Psychologists and psychiatrists pay considerably more than that. Because I own a house and some materials, I wouldn't want to do without it, but the insurance itself doesn't really quell my anxiety about being sued. The fact is that if I were to be even unjustly accused of sexual impropriety or some other ethical breach, it might very well destroy my practice. Personally I consider there to be three more important means of insuring oneself against malpractice suits. One is in being personable, straightforward, and careful in the work. People normally don't sue people who are conscientious, honest, and personable. Another is to nurture other possibilities for pursuing another career. Frankly, I believe psychotherapy is a fragile career that is just an unjust accusation away from disaster. I take great comfort in the fantasy of being free to pursue teaching or coaching. I have dabbled in both occupations for years, and although my preference is to remain a therapist, I would welcome the opportunity to dive into another vocation. What I wouldn't welcome would be having it imposed upon me by a wrongly marred reputation and the financial hardship such a change would cause. Plus, I really like being a therapist. I intend to remain a therapist by being careful, honest, and ethical. The third and most important way to protect against malpractice is to never promise success. By not promising successful therapy, those who fail do not have grounds to sue on breach of promise. I, of course, do not think we'll fail, but I certainly do not guarantee success.

Most people who become therapists have a strong introverted component to their personality. For introverts to work in the deep privacy of counseling there is an inherent psychological pitfall. One can easily become socially isolated. Thus, I consider an essential ingredient of my work to be a good collegial atmosphere. I want other people around me. I like to have a close therapist colleague whom I trust and respect. It helps me immensely to be able to say on occasion, "Wow! I just had a session that wiped me out." Or "I saw a client yesterday who is a joy to be working with." It is important to me to share few details about what happened, except that which happens to me. A therapist colleague can understand without needing details. I also love to keep good relations with the building's mechanics or janitors, for I used to do that kind of work and I love to talk shop with them. Plus, I keep strong ties with a few people who love to talk and participate in sports. I run with a group of friends once or twice a week and play basketball, softball, or golf once a week. I can share with any of them my joys and struggles. Hence, I think that any structure needs to give a therapist enough flexibility to be informally collegial, have fun, and take time off.

The issue of staffing clients and keeping abreast of one's work is important. In my experience there are three kinds of clients one encounters: (1) garden variety problems, (2) unusually intense, complicated, and/or interesting problems, and (3) extreme problems. The most usual client is the garden variety—that is, a routine or mildly neurotic person. These are simply problems one is quite familiar with, problems common to the experienced professional. For the beginning therapist, however, almost all problems are new and out of the ordinary. The unusual problems come in two varieties: those that are simply fascinating, and those that are confusing, befuddling. These are problems that are fun and/or essential to talk with another professional about. An example might be a highly successful man who is a closet transvestite whose mother killed herself when he was very young and whose father was an alcoholic who made a million dollars through illegal means and whose wife has a compulsive spending problem. After being introduced to such a client, a therapist needs a place to say, "Wow! What a story!" The third type of problem is the suicide threatening client, the raging alcoholic, the abused family, the psychotic—problems that seriously tax the lone therapist. Such problems are best dealt with in consultation with colleagues.

I find that verbally staffing everyone is very time consuming and boring. A staff that tries to run every intake through an intake conference usually has either inordinately long meetings or many persons simply slide through unstaffed. The best system for a consultative intake process has three elements to it. First, every client should be written up in a standard format. This should be a thorough process, but not take much time to do. With a familiar format, an intake write-up should take no more than 10-15 minutes. If it takes much longer, not all of them will get done. Secondly, a senior clinician supervisor should be responsible for reading every intake and returning comments back to the intake counselor. This supervisor should make a disposition of the case in one of two directions: the case should be assigned to the intake counselor without it going through the case conference, or the case should be sent to the next case conference for the whole staff to read and help with the disposition and treatment plan. Thirdly, cases sent to the intake conference should be dealt with carefully and efficiently. An intake case conference that spends more than 20 minutes on a client is being poorly managed. It is a mistake to drag out intake staffings because (1) bored staff say stupid things and (2) it discourages staff from bringing new cases to the conferences (there won't be time for them anyway, we rationalize) and therefore encourages staff members to not promptly inform the system of intakes.

Intakes are for the primary purpose of properly establishing a relationship. Secondarily, their purpose is to set up a treatment plan. Many clinics see the intake to be primarily this second purpose. That may be a major difference I have with some clinicians. With intake priorities in the order I suggest, the work of therapy is treated properly as art first, technique or science second.

Work hours are an important decision for the therapist to make. If clients had their way all the time, most full-time therapists would be working four nights a week and on

Saturdays. From the outset, one must establish one's own hours and not be easily seduced away from them. Myself, I see clients preferably during the day, but I reserve two nights a week for appointments. I don't have Saturday or Sunday appointments. Someday I hope to have the confidence to cut down to one night a week. I do not dislike working at night, but I do miss some of the things others get to do in the evenings. However, I do not like to turn referrals away. I prefer to have hours available to those who seek my help. Occasionally I have such a strong caseload that I have to place people on "waiting list", but that's rare. Even well established clinicians need referrals. When one is starting out or not fully confident of one's level of demand, client convenient hours, that is, hours convenient for the 9-5 worker, are an important consideration.

Referral Structure

Every therapist needs people he or she can refer clients to. Some cases simply are not within our ability to handle. One way to look at the kinds of clients one will need to refer elsewhere is to have an understanding of what one's own subspecialties are within the psychotherapeutic specialty. Here are some of the clear subspecialties:

1) marital therapy,
2) family therapy,
3) child play therapy,
4) adolescent therapy,
5) psychiatry,
6) addiction treatment (which has subspecialties within it, such as, eating disorders, alcohol and drug treatment, sexual addictions, compulsive spending, adult children of alcoholics, families of alcoholics or addicts),

7) self-help group work,
8) educational testing,
9) phobias treatment.

In fact, in this age of the expert, there's probably a sub-specialist in just about anything. One with specialized training could claim that no one not similarly trained should treat certain types of problems. In my opinion that is always a partial truth. Sub-specialists do have the advantage of being familiar with problems that would be strange to others, but therapy is more art than science, and no amount of expertise nullifies that. The good therapist is primarily artist, and in art technique is secondary.

I am a pastoral counselor with sub-specialties in working with individual adults, adolescents, and children (in play therapy), marital therapy, and family therapy. I work with mild cases of panic disorders and like to do work with dreams. I also do some work with adult therapy groups, particularly ones that focus on dreams. For needs beyond my skill I refer to particular psychiatrists, addiction treatment programs, child and adolescent inpatient treatment programs, adult inpatient treatment programs, educational and learning specialists, and all of the Twelve-Step programs. However, I treat probably 95% of those who seek my help myself, using my referral sources for support for the therapy I am doing.

CHAPTER SIX
THE OFFICE ENVIRONMENT

The arrangement and decoration of one's office is worth paying close attention to, for within the office is the implicit structure that determines the comfort level of the therapeutic relationship. Thus, what follows are the details necessary in setting up a good, comfortable office.

Climate control needs to be within the office itself. Sitting hour after hour in an office without physical exertion is not the normal level of activity most people have within a building. Therapists often feel cold in winter and cold in summer from the air conditioning. It is so nice to be able to set one's own thermostat. I have seen people in offices where I have had my own thermostat and others where I have not. In the latter I kept a small space heater, a fan, a spare sweater, and a lap blanket in case I feel or my client feels uncomfortable.

A carpet or rug makes an office feel much warmer and softer. It invites trust and vulnerability. Soft lighting does the same thing. An overhead light is too much like an interrogation room. Lamps are essential to a good therapist's office. Soft chairs are in this category, too. The office needs to say, "Relax, you can get comfortable in here."

I prefer to have three chairs. I have one chair that is mine, one that I can gently rock in and gives me good back support. Therapists are notorious for having back problems because of sitting for hours in poor chairs with poor posture. I have another chair that seats only one person and another chair that is a couch. I prefer a three person couch because couples can sit at opposite ends of a couch and easily see one another when they talk. I've had offices that are too small for a full size couch, so I've settled for a loveseat. I like to have at least four places to sit for two reasons. One is because I often have four persons in my office (if I have five or more, I pull in an extra chair or two). Another is because I like clients to have a choice of seating. Sometimes I learn something about them by where they sit, especially couples or families. One family of three came in and they all sat uncomfortably on the three person couch with the mother between the son and step-father. Towards the end of the session I observed that they seemed uncomfortable in that arrangement, and they exclaimed that they were. The mother then said, "This is how I always am in the family. I'm the mediator, and I don't like it."

I like to have a small desk in my office. I keep mine near the door so that I can go to it at the end of the session in a way that suggests we are moving out of the sanctuary, and also because I can see clients arrive easier. I do not like to have a large desk, for that seems to me to change the softness of the room. It makes it seem more like an office than a sanctuary.

This word sanctuary is the key concept in creating a counseling space. A sanctuary is a haven from the storm, a place of retreat, a place of peace, a place where one can relax and be vulnerable. The key question one should ask in arranging one's office is "How can I make this space be a sanctuary?" I also think sanctuary is a better word than retreat center because of its implication of holiness. The deepest quality of the therapeutic relationship has a mysterious and transcendent quality to it. Treating the creation of the space with reverence is only right. In a good counseling office clients will often take off their shoes, ostensibly to get more comfortable, but I believe such acts have symbolic significance. The shadow side is that this is often a subtle and act of seductivity, albeit almost always as innocent as a child's sensuousness is slightly seductive. The holy side is that this is like Moses removing his shoes before the burning bush because it was holy ground.

I keep records locked away and normally out of sight of my clients. That is my business, my way of remembering things that might be helpful to them for me to remember. They do not need to be reminded that I am a clinician. They need me to be as helpful as a clinician while available like a friend.

I carefully place my clocks so that I do not make it obvious that I'm keeping track of the time. I want to be able to see the clock through the corner of my eye and not have to sneak a look at it. Getting caught checking the clock is rather common, but it seems a bit impolite and is really not my client's business. Keeping track of our time is my business, so I prefer to do it discreetly. I like my office to have at least two clocks in it, and I have a watch in case of power outages.

Some therapists prefer simple, landscape types of pictures. I prefer evocative artwork. Not harshly so, but art that evokes some association. Anything the client says about anything in my office I consider to be information he or she is sharing with me to help me understand. I have a picture of my family in my office, too, but I don't like to display it too prominently, for I think it is best that my private life be my private life, just as my business is not their business. I hang my credentialing papers and diplomas in a somewhat discrete location, that is, near the desk or door. Sometimes I think they're there just for my big head, but I believe they make an important statement about my persona, my role. They remind clients that I am friendly, but not a friend. I have appropriate professional detachment and training to be of help.

I keep books in my office for two purposes. One is because I agree with Voltaire who once wrote that "a room without books is like a body without a soul." I love books. Another is because I refer to them often in sessions. I loan books and I read passages in sessions. The books I keep in my office are almost all psychologically and theologically oriented, although I do have some books of poetry as well.

I keep a voice recorder in my office for two purposes. One is because it's a great play therapy tool. Children will often talk more openly into a microphone than face to face. Another is because I occasionally tape sessions to take to a consultant. Of course when I do my clients or supervisees know why I'm taping and give me permission to do so, and the recorder is always out in the open. I would never tape secretly. That would be a gross breach of ethics as well as a gross breach of trust.

I keep my own calendar, and I keep it with me all the time. I don't let anyone look at it. I keep it closed unless I'm using it. I tend to write small, so a six inch calendar that fits in my back pocket is perfect for me. I always put the phone numbers of a new client next to the name when I schedule the first session, which helps me find their numbers on some occasions, and I keep a monthly client list with phone numbers in a pocket of the calendar cover. One of my worst professional fears is losing my calendar, for I seek to guard my clients' identities stringently.

Telephone Answering

Telephone answering is an area where care must be taken. There are five put-offs to phone answering. One is having to listen to lots of rings. Good businesses stress the importance of answering the phone by the second ring. Even though I've been taught to wait for six rings when calling someone, I usually wait only four. Two rings and an answer is good business. A long recorded message is annoying. I know who I've called and only need verification that I've dialed the right number. I also know how to leave messages on an answering machine and don't need to be told how to do it. The reason why I sometimes don't leave a message is almost always because of too long of a message. Answering services often identify themselves poorly. When an answering service answers "Dr. McDonald's office," one is inclined to think one has reach the office itself. I'm annoyed when I find that I haven't. The only good answer from an answering services, in my opinion, is in the form of "Dr. McDonald's answering service." Personally I don't use answering services. I prefer a good answering machine or voice mail. Another put-off is being put on hold or call-waiting. Call waiting essentially means that the person calling in has priority over the person on the line. It may be convenient, it may even be necessary, but it is annoying. To place someone on hold should always be apologized for. Finally, an tardy return of messages is a put-off. Calls should be returned within two hours if at all possible. Again, it's good business.

The reason why I prefer an answering machine or voice mail when a receptionist is not available is because it's so simple. Thus, I keep my messages simple, short, and I check the machine very often. I have also found that a machine that has a time of call marker on it is helpful, and spending the extra bucks for a better than average machine or voice mail is money well spent.

CHAPTER SEVEN
PUBLIC RELATIONS

How one presents oneself publicly has a major bearing on the success of one's practice. This is, of course, the marketing of one's practice, and thus one can approach it in a purely businesslike manner and advertise. Advertisement works too. I once worked for a large hospital clinic that had a half page ad in the Yellow Pages. We received a good number of calls as a result of that ad, but two out of three of them did not show up for the first appointment. Mass advertisement has the tendency to attract persons in acute crises, and three days later when the crises has abated somewhat, the reason they called has also abated, and they cancel or don't show.

Anyone in practice receives many letters and brochures from successful practitioners who boast that they can turn a struggling practice into a half-million dollar business in six months. I've never tried one of these approaches, but when I'm insecure about my practice, I've often been tempted. And I've often asked for the "three free copies" they offer. What I've found is helpful but not salvation. Success still depends on good quality, hard work, and good exposure.

So I market myself through seven methods. *First* is volunteer work. There are two types of volunteer work. One is purely for self-satisfaction, like coaching sports. Another is the volunteering of one's expertise—doing some free counseling. I've found over the years that the self-satisfying volunteer work draws me a few referrals, but, more importantly, broadens my experience and sense of self-worth. I'm a better therapist because of these activities. Volunteering my expertise will pay off with referrals. One of my colleagues calls this "stewardship." It's hard to give away one's professional services, especially when one needs more money, but in the long run it builds community respect and loyalty from persons who make referrals. For example, I volunteered for about seven years at the Church Health Center in Memphis, seeing the so-called "working poor" (people who earn low wages with no benefits and are therefore excluded from the health care system). The work was usually short term and most of the clients had chronic problems, but the staff there came to believe in my high level of caring and commitment as well as my ability to help people. Many on their staff came to me for help, paying a fair fee. After seven years of receiving their referrals, I was hired by them.

Second, educational programs are an excellent way to market oneself. There is an art of presenting materials and oneself that draws referrals. Basically I believe one can accomplish this by (1) choosing material to present that one loves to share, material that is vital to one's own life; and (2) being real, open, and a good listener. I present educational programs in two settings: groups that are seeking a professional presentation, and a planned and advertised seminar. I also charge at least a minimal amount for these activities. I believe that education works best when it is not simply a gift but a reciprocal arrangement, that is, I'll teach and you pay. Teaching is professional activity that should be presented in a way parallel to one's professional activity, which is on a fee basis. I seek to demonstrate in an educational format how I work. I've often said that my best teaching is "counseling in public." By that I mean that I do my best when leading discussions, fielding concerns and opinions much like I do in family or marital counseling.

Third, public speaking is similar to educational programs, but it is usually very short in comparison, and thus I seek to present the best summary of how I think about a subject in a way that touches the audience as deeply as possible. I consider this parallel to preaching, and thus often follow a sermonic format, usually without the sectarian or overtly doctrinal material. Thus, in my own public speaking I tell stories, sing songs, and share insights into their meaning. I seek to enchant, for enchantment reaches most deeply into the recesses of our souls. Stories and music are a great means of enchantment. Plus, stories are a means of holding a mirror up to ourselves, making us feel simultaneously vulnerable and safe, which is exactly what I want my clients to feel.

A colleague of mine used to say that displaying musical talents turned clients away, because they might feel intimidated by talent beyond their own. However, I've found that talent is only a means to delivering a message, and if the message is evocative and meaningful, a talented presentation draws an audience towards the presenter even more effectively.

Fourth, professional hobnobbing is essential in one's practice, both at the guild level, and the local level. There are a lot of good professionals out there who make good friends and colleagues. We need their help, and the good ones know that they need our help too. I attend professional workshops not only to learn something, but also to meet other professionals. I put on a happy face and reach out to them. I also call on some and get together over lunch with them. These relationships pay off.

Fifth, I write about a hour each day, a craft that rarely gets me any referrals or money, but helps me think more clearly and may eventually be a part of my success. I write for the long run.

Sixth, business cards are cheap and essential. I give them out often, and I've never known whether or not they make much of a difference, but if I get one referral every year from a stray card, one session more than pays for the cards.

Seventh, marketing experts suggest that signs are the most effective and cheapest way to advertise. A hundred dollar sign placed in a highly visible location will get your name out for less cost and effort than anything.

Finally I end this chapter with a pastoral counselor's, Rev. William Scar, list of 12 things one should do to insure clinical success. He calls them the "internal marketing" of psychotherapy, which means the commitment to quality and outreach one conveys to clients and referring professionals.

WILLIAM SCAR'S 12 POINTS OF INTERNAL MARKETING

1. The belief that God has sent each and every person who comes to us for help
2. An attitude of strength and confidence that there are always answers to problems;
3. Clear and consistent management of the financial and scheduling boundaries of the counseling process
4. Immediate attention to diagnosis
5. Rapid and effective response in the handling of every area of a case
6. Demonstrated concern for every area of the client's life
7. Ongoing attention to the symbols of the faith journey of the client
8. Active communication with the person's medical doctors and pastor or rabbi

9. Referral for medical care if persons have no physician or whenever indications warrant
10. Inclusion of family members wherever and whenever possible in the therapeutic process
11. The establishment and monitoring of behavioral goals for the near and long term
12. The conscious and expressed recognition of the stages or process of the therapy, including shifts in the role of the therapist (AAPC "Newsletter, 1992).

Many of these ideas will be more fully expressed in the following chapters of this book.

PART TWO
THE RELATIONSHIP SANCTUARY

CHAPTER EIGHT
WHEN THE CLIENT CALLS

The therapist's office meets a crisis with every phone call from a potential client. Depending on how the therapist responds to the call, that office will either be a work site or become a sanctuary. Poor management of the initial contact with a client keeps the office just an office. Good management transforms the office into a sanctuary—a safe, sacred place where healing and change can truly begin. Obviously, I am concerned with encouraging the latter. We shall begin with the initial phone call.

The initial phone call from a potential client is loaded with meaning and prior baggage. Most importantly, there is a load of personal pain and shame brought to that phone call. It is very hard to make that initial phone call to a therapist. Most people are in great pain when they decide to call. Because to call a therapist means an admission of one's inability to handle one's problems within the scope of one's personal life structure, it is often a shame-filled act. The point of view of nearly everyone calling a therapist is essentially, "I'm ashamed to admit it, but I can't seem to solve this problem. I need help." Fortunately the act of calling for help is also the most important turning point in the finding of solutions to problems, for one best finds solutions from a position of humility, and humility is but a short step away from humiliation or shame.

Prior to the call the prospective client will have heard of the therapist or clinic in some manner. Whether it be through the Yellow Pages or via a friend or former client, the source of the referral has some unpredictable bearing on the contact and future therapy. The most important aspect of this impression is that potential clients project onto the therapist some of their deepest hopes for healing and help. Even the most suspicious and paranoid clients will not call a therapist unless there is within them some hope for transformation that they want the therapist to be a bridge to. The client is like a person stuck on a deserted island, starving, and the therapist is to the client like a rescue ship. Thus the therapist is initially handed some godlike projections. We are expected to have some savior-like qualities. It is sometimes easy to deflect these projections with comments that humble oneself: like, "I'm only human," or "I can only help as far as you are able to cooperate with the process." But in spite of the fact that these comments are true, they are not helpful at the outset of therapy. One of the most important health-giving processes in the human spirit is the desire to commune with the gods. When a client approaches a therapist as a god, it is most importantly a reverent approach that puts the client into a transcendent realm where openness, trust, hope, and love are the dominant urgings. These four qualities are at the essence of health. One of the most important tasks of the therapist is to absorb these projections until it is appropriate to turn them back to the client where one can recognize that of God within oneself.

Initial Conversation

Elemental to any good business conversation is the identification of the one being called. A simple, "Hello," like we might be accustomed to answering at home is inappropriate at work. "This is Dr. McDonald," must follow the salutation, or the predictable next question of the caller will be "To whom am I speaking?" No one should have to ask that question on a business call.

I have notepaper and pencils next to my phone for jotting down information during any call. I try not to waste anyone's time with fumbling for a pad and pencil, just as I dislike it when someone does that to me. When 99% of business calls include taking down messages, to not be prepared to take messages is rude. I also seek to have my calendar with me as I take a call, for I'll need to refer to my calendar for 75% of all calls I receive.

Because I'm in session most of my working time, I usually speak with clients on return calls. I identify myself by saying, "This is Dr. McDonald returning so-and-so's call." I used to refer to myself without the "Dr.", saying simply "Ron McDonald," because I thought it was best to work on a first name basis, but as I've gotten obviously older I've found that most people prefer to call me "Dr. McDonald" whether I like it or not. It has become obvious to me that being called "Dr. McDonald" rather than "Ron" is a sign of respect that many people feel more comfortable with. However, I certainly don't mind when someone is comfortable with and prefers a first name relationship. I also used to leave off the "Dr." because I thought such an identification might arouse suspicion from a client's family or friends. The client might have called me hoping to talk with me with no one knowing he or she had called, but I've found that most people think "Dr." means medical doctor, which is not usually threatening. If the one who answers asks for more identification, I simply add, "from the Church Health Center," which further protects the client from others being told that a therapist is calling. What I clearly try to avoid is identifying myself as a therapist or counselor to anyone other than the client. The fact that he or she has called for the help of a therapist is confidential. (Of course, with my name, when I say "Ron McDonald" many who answer the phone think I'm a prank caller anyway—but I did have the name first! That's just what I have to live with.)

I seek to make three primary assessments quickly in an initial conversation: (1) what is the reason for the call?, (2) what is the level of distress?, and (3) what parties are involved.

Generally there are only two reasons for the initial call. One is to get an impression of the therapist and decide whether or not to set up an appointment. If this is the case, I make sure I have at least five minutes to talk. Usually such a conversation begins with a statement like this: "My friend referred me to you, and I'm calling to see what kind of counseling you do and if I should set up an appointment with you." If I have less than five minutes available, I will immediately say, "I have an appointment scheduled to begin in about a minute, but at 11:00 I will be free to talk with you for a while. Can I call you back then when we'll have more time?" Then we begin negotiating the right time. If I have the time available now, I respond to their question about me first: "I am a pastoral counselor." (If asked what a pastoral counselor is, I add, "I'm a minister who has received specialized training and degrees in psychotherapy.") "I work mostly with individual adults, marriage and family problems, and I also work with teenagers and children." Then I add, "What kind of problem were you referred to me for?" Some persons will ask me more about myself and my training, which I answer factually, but usually the conversation will shift to their problem. My purpose is not to set up an appointment, but to help them decide whether or not to set one up. They will make this decision based upon their impression of me, whether or not they feel heard and understood, and practicality. Thus, I want their impression of me to be that I am warm, accessible, straightforward, and professional. I want to respect the courage it took to call me, and convey that respect by listening very carefully. It helps me to jot down notes as they talk, particularly names they mention. Being able to call by name a person they have mentioned, next to authenticity, is next best way to gently enter a potential client's world. Ministers, coaches, and teachers have long known the tremendous importance of knowing names.

Presently I work under two structures. When receiving a call from someone referred to my private practice, I let the prospective client know that I am open to negotiation. I say, "I charge $75 a session, but that is slightly negotiable, if necessary." Some therapists simply say, "My fee is _____", but I believe in saying what is true about my fee, which is that it is negotiable, even if I might be a tough negotiator. In fact, virtually all therapists' fees are negotiable. Why not say so? If the caller comments that he or she will need a fee adjustment, I say that I usually don't go under $60 a session and wait to hear if that is still prohibitive. If it is I suggest that we look at alternative ways of working together, one being inviting them to considering becoming a patient at the nonprofit organization I work for where I see people on a sliding fee basis. When insurance issues are broached, I ask the name of their insurance company. If it's not one that generally reimburses for my services, I say, "I am covered by a few insurance carriers. I suggest you call your insurance company and check. If I'm not covered, they can recommend therapists who are, and I would be willing to hear those names and recommend someone I might know."

The other structure I work for, the Church Health Center, is a not-for-profit holistic medical clinic for working people who cannot afford health insurance. When receiving a referral call from clinic patients they will usually tell me they were referred by one of our doctors for a particular problem, saying, "Dr. _____ suggested I give you a call." I normally respond by asking, "And you agreed that it would be a good idea?" I want to know if the person agrees with the referral, if he or she owns the decision.

The second reason for the initial call is simply to set up an appointment, and if the caller is clear that this is a personal and an appropriate objective, I tell prospective clients my approximate hours: "I see people during the weekdays and two evenings a week." I want them to understand that the appointment time and fee are flexible, even though the flexibility itself hasn't yet been defined. If I happen to have a full schedule, I will explain my limitations: "I do not have a time available this week, and have only two hours available for next week." Or "I have only one appointment available this week at _____ time." They deserve an accurate impression of my availability. I will also tell them where my office is, so they'll know how far they'll have to travel.

I have learned to not be too flexible with my schedule. I've learned that people prefer to seek help from someone who is busy helping others. Furthermore, if I am too accommodating I find myself feeling angry—not a good way to start a counseling relationship. If I have to be more flexible than a client, I resent it, and part of my job as therapist is to protect my clients from my resentments.

However, I am particularly flexible with a prospective client who calls in the midst of considerable stress and crisis. Very few persons call a therapist expecting immediate help, but some call in such a crisis that prompt help is appropriate. Although I often am mistaken, when I pick up a high level of stress, I will try to find a time slot within two days, even if I have to change my schedule some. I am not an emergency counseling service or crisis counselor by design, but I believe every therapist has to do some of this. And it is still true that an occasional crisis case is exciting and exhilarating to deal with. However, even for the person in the worse crisis I find it therapeutically helpful to not meet him or her that day. I usually find the next available time other than today. It fosters patience and the necessary ability to calm down and find inward ways to cope with stress.

I seek to know who the parties are that should be involved in counseling. I will ask, "Is this a problem of yours alone, or is there another person involved who might want to come in also?" If the caller says, "Well, I do have problems with my spouse, but I'd like to see you myself," I'll ask more questions, sometimes asserting that "My experience is that when a spouse is involved like you are describing, it would be best for us to meet together at least the first time." I'll ask the caller to talk with his or her spouse and call me back after the invitation is made. Sometimes, though, I'll consent to seeing the caller alone first with the knowledge that we might include the spouse later. Some callers will ask me if I think they should come with their spouse. Hearing such a question leads me to explore the issue of individual or conjoint treatment with the caller. I usually prefer conjoint therapy if there is some question, but not always, especially when one party sounds unmotivated. Unmotivated clients are not much fun to work with, and they often undermine the working tone of a session. I'd rather work with motivated clients and let the absent spouse or other family member decide on one's own if he or she wants to come.

I ask callers who referred them. I want to know that mainly for myself. Keeping abreast of referral sources and thanking them is a business necessity. However, I do not talk with referral sources about their referral without permission from the client.

Finally, I end each phone call with a brief summary of the appointment time and place: "I'll see you at 10 o'clock Tuesday, May 21, at my office." I get enough intermittent reinforcement for that to know that I avoid 4 or 5 mistakes a year with that recheck on the appointment.

I don't trust my memory. I always write appointments into my calendar immediately. Well, almost always, for about once every two years I find someone showing up to my surprise after I somehow didn't get their name down in my book.

The last thing I do after an appointment is made with a prospective client is to privately say a brief prayer for our work together. I want God's help.

CHAPTER NINE
THE STRUCTURE OF THE FIRST SESSION

First Impressions

Children's book writers are well aware of the importance of the beginning of each picture book. There is an implicit contract that is presented from the first page of the book. From page one the reader should know whether or not this is a story that follows realistic rules, whether it is a story with animals portrayed like humans, whether it is a fairy tale that includes specials powers or abilities. Once that contract is established, if the story does not follow those rules, the reader is thrown into confusion and will usually feel cheated. For example, if a story is set in Memphis, Tennessee, unless there is some illusion to the Memphis Zoo, if a tiger suddenly enters into the story, the reader will recoil in disbelief and the story loses its credibility.

The beginning of therapy has such a contract. The client should be able to expect a few social amenities from the therapist: that directions will be accurate, parking will be relatively convenient, entry into the office environment will be easy, the office environment will be reasonably comfortable, and the office environment will be private. Thus, I am carefully clear about directions and make sure that those who will relate first with my clients are courteous and non-intrusive.

Some clients will still get lost and enter with complaints about getting here, but since I've been careful and clear I know I am seeing evidence of their problem, their way of negotiating through the world.

I always remind myself of the name of clients before greeting them, then I include their names in my greeting. I greet clients by their first name, offer them a handshake upon first meeting, then say, "I'm Ron McDonald, and you may call me 'Ron' or 'Dr. McDonald', whichever you prefer."

Handshakes are an interesting barometer of mood, at least for men. There are aggressive handshakes, passive handshakes, and handshakes among equals. The former two convey insecurity and, often, underlying depression. I take careful, unspoken note of this expression of selfhood.

I seek to convey a message of security and openness to clients as they enter my domain. My fundamental position is "I set the frame; you determine the action." Thus, I seek to put clients at ease from the beginning, inviting them in, letting them know what they can call me, and suggesting where they sit. As quickly as possible I want them to get comfortable so we can begin our work.

My opening words into the work at hand are of two types. If I have gathered information from a referral source about the clients, I share that information. I want them to know that I don't keep secrets or seek outside information about them, nor will I be checking out the veracity of their story outside of the context of our work together. Thus, I might begin a session by saying, "What I have heard about you is that your father died a few months ago and Dr. _____ thinks that you are having a tough time." Then I add what is my usual opening statement: "What brings you here, and how can I be of help?" I assume that clients know better than a referral source why and how they need help. I want to hear it from the horse's mouth.

The Beginning Statement

The first thing a client says to the therapist might very well be the most important thing said. If a client says, "Gee, it's cold outside," that might be the best hint as to what the core issue of therapy will be about. The therapist should listen carefully to these initial comments, for they are always metaphors into the unconscious track the client will take throughout the session. And the first comment of the first session has particular significance, for it will be the metaphor that points to the core issue of the whole therapy experience.

For example, a woman came to my office, and when I opened the door, she said, "I came here because the other door is locked. Is this where I'm supposed to be?" I merely answered "Yes," but not without thinking to myself of the metaphorical power of those two sentences: I am locked out; I am lost.

For this reason it is best that the therapist as much as possible seek to say as little as possible upon being introduced to a new client. "I'm Ron McDonald. Come in." Then I wait for a few seconds to see what response might come.

Sometimes the response is nonverbal. A client might stand in the middle of the room and appeared confused about where to sit down. I note that: I am confused; I don't know where to rest myself; I'm trying to be polite. I will not, however, interpret or conjecture on the response. The relationship is too new to share my "powers of observation" (that's a joke!). Instead I deal only with the obvious surface need and say, "Please have a seat on the couch. I'll sit in the chair opposite you."

I have my favorite chair to sit in, but I don't protect it all the time. Some clients come in and from the start sit in that chair, and since I've set up clocks in my room from every angle, I don't mind sitting on one of the two couches. In fact, I kind of like the change once in a while. However, I usually do claim my favorite chair, for it's better on my back than the couches, and I have a chronically sore back. I listen best when I'm comfortable.

A Guiding Principle

I'll underline my guiding model for a good first session: listen, question, comment.

A number of years ago I was working in a day care center as a part-time teacher while also attending graduate school classes. One of my classes was a "field work" experience called Clinical Pastoral Education (C.P.E.) where I worked as a hospital chaplain. I was having problems at the school with helping children iron out conflicts when a comment made to me in C.P.E. made sense in the school setting. I had been told by my C.P.E. supervisor that I sometimes thought I understood the patients before I really could be sure I did. Perhaps, I thought, I could be doing the same thing with children in conflict with one another.

The next argument I was called upon to mediate between children I approached differently. Rather than seeking to judge right from wrong and hand out a just decision, I started from the assumption that I needed to be sure I understood before commenting on anything. "What happened?" I asked.

"Joey pushed me," Susy answered.

"Why did you push Susy?" I asked Joey.

"She wouldn't let me play."

"Why wouldn't you let Joey play?" I asked Susy.

"Because he just came in here without asking."

Joey responded, "I did too and you didn't answer me."

"I didn't hear you," Susy replied. "Do you want to be the father?"

"OK."

And they went on playing with me scratching my head in awe of how easily they had worked that out.

Until it made sense to me that smart as I am I'm not smart enough to understand very easily, I wasn't much help. I've learned that the smartest thing for me to do is to assume I'm too ignorant to comment. In other words, I "play dumb". I keep asking the obvious question, and when I finally am sure I understand, my clients normally go on to something else. And if they haven't, a comment might be in order to help them see what I think I see.

Although the experienced therapist might be able to discern core problems rather quickly, the hardest yet most helpful listening begins out of humble ignorance and a trust that all that is presented is in fact connected to the core problem, even if it's hard to understand.

By humble ignorance I mean that the appropriate posture for the therapist is not "I am the expert," but "I don't know." Behind the questioning process is the assumption that "I don't quite understand." The therapist who takes this position of humility is the therapist who can help the most.

In fact, what makes a good therapist is the willingness to let one's clients teach one how to do therapy. Stated another way, if you're willing to let your clients teach you how to be a good therapist, you'll eventually become a good therapist.

I have learned from clients that (1) clients come prepared whether they know it or not, (2) clients continue their therapeutic work after the session, and (3) the therapist's job is to not get in their way. Let me address this.

Client Work Prior to the Session

Each new client comes into each session prepared. Even when the client suggests that he or she is unprepared, preparation is simply beyond consciousness. Sometimes a client comes in and says, "I don't know what to talk about. I had to hurry so much to get here that I didn't prepared myself." I hear such a statement in this way: "I am lost. I prepared myself by staying away from my usual habit of planning the session. And when I don't plan ahead, I lose my ability to know where I am, how to carry on, and what to do. I get out of touch with my emotions. That is what I want to deal with today."

Another client comes to a session with a rigid agenda: "I've got three things to talk about and I want your advice on them." I hear such a statement on two levels: first, I'm glad he or she is consciously prepared. Our work might be easier. Secondly, I wonder to myself if an issue before us is control, particularly a fear of letting one's emotional or unconscious life move in a new direction.

In either case the task of the therapist is to gently understand—listen, question, and comment. The assumption is that the client is prepared whether admitted or not.

Client Work After the Session

Some of the most important work of therapy occurs just after the session has ended. It is important that the therapist realize that a session does not end for the client like it does for the therapist. The client moves through a good session into a fast flowing steam of unconscious and conscious material. Much will continue to bubble to the surface, giving insight and understanding outside of the therapy hour. Particularly just after the session, there is often a great deal happening. The ride or walk home is usually a pensive and important time. I often ask a client how he or she felt or continued to process the last session, often receiving much information in the reporting of that continued work.

The Therapist's Job

The therapist's job is most importantly to let-be. The therapist's job is an hour long. If the therapist continues to work consistently on the client's issues beyond that hour, then there is a high degree of counter-transference. The therapist's job is confined to the session. It's that simple.

Filling in the Gaps in the Client's Story

Sometime into the first session I need to find out some factual information about the client—a kind of fleshing out of the bare bones that I can now see. Sometimes I'm very thorough and directive; mostly I follow various lines of questioning that helps me better understand one or two aspects of a client's history. I usually don't feel the need to do a thorough history-taking early in the relationship. Some therapists do, both because it quells their anxiety and/or because they are excellent at sifting through facts and discerning core issues and complexes. I personally can get somewhat overwhelmed with too many facts, so I try to gather what helps me understand. Part of why I gather some more facts is to help me remember the person better. In the next chapter I'll expand on this need.

There is an important story that has greatly influenced my understanding of the importance of remembering. In Greek mythology, travelers on their way to Athens were abducted and strapped to Procrustes' bed. If they were too short, they were stretched to fit. If they were too tall, they were cut down to size. Then they were released to continue their journey. Most were wounded.

Part of the healing process of psychotherapy is to go back to those wounding experiences—our Procrustian beds—and find our lost parts or reattach our joints as they were meant to be. In other words, we must go back to where we were dis-membered and re-member.

Remembering is *very* important!

Recommendations

For the first 30 minutes of the first session I will have spent my time listening, questioning, and, to myself, making a diagnosis (which I will address in the next chapter). With about 15 minutes left I interrupt the conversation and say, "Let me give you some feedback." And that's just what I do.

Moving out of professional language into lay language, I share my diagnosis. I seek to convey my understanding, insight, and some possible new responses to the presenting problem. I seek to do this in five minutes, then we will have about ten minutes to process what I have said. (I used to let clients go on for 45 or 50 minutes in the first session, then offer my recommendations and allow for process time after that, allowing an initial session to go about an hour and twenty minutes. I don't like to do that anymore, partly because as a more experienced therapist I can diagnose a problem more quickly now, partly because I have admitted my listening limits better now than I used to. I'm not a good listener much past 45-50 minutes. I don't get onto therapists who have extended first sessions because I think it's part of one's maturation as a therapist, but in the long run, therapists who spend more time with clients are not necessarily helping the process. It's a nice thing to do, but good therapy doesn't depend on the therapist being nice.)

Here's what I might say to someone. "What I understand is that you have been very confused lately, to the point where you've come here wondering if you are crazy. But as you've talked, you actually have some clear ideas about what's going on, and even think that you're not the central problem—that the relationship is the real problem. You don't appear to be blaming of your spouse, but you are angry with him/her and you've been shouldering much of the blame for the chaos and craziness yourself.

"Yet in spite of this confusion, you actually have a fairly clear vision of what needs to be done and what the real problem is. What you haven't had is the courage to lay claim to your position. As you've shared this with me it appears that you are convincing yourself that you need to do some things you've been talking yourself out of to avoid the conflict. But the conflict hasn't been going away. In fact, it's gotten worse, to the point where you can no longer avoid it."

At this point I usually add, "Am I making sense to you?" If the clients says yes, I ask how. If the client says no, I ask what hasn't made sense. After we have processed this for a while, I usually say, "I have a recommendation. Would you like to hear it?" I ask that question for two reasons. One is because there's no sense making a recommendation to a person if he or she still has more to say. The other is because I want to know if the client is willing to move towards me. Edwin Friedman was fond of saying that no one can hear us unless he or she is moving towards us. Of course, 99% of the time, the client says, "Yes, I do." At that I typically say, "From what I've heard from you it might be helpful for you to do . . ." I am very careful to not say, "Try this." I do not trust my recommendations that much. I think I have some good ideas, but my view of the situation is rather myopic. Plus, I don't want a client to go home and say, "My therapist told me to do this." Half the time clients do that anyway, but that's because they hear it that way, not because I tell them what to do. I would guess that 90% of the time a client says, "My therapist told me to do this," the therapist merely made a suggestion or illuminated an option, or the therapist mirrored back to the client something he or she wanted to do. "I hear you saying that you'd like to stand up to him," is translated into, "My therapist told me to tell you off."

There is an interesting difference in how I talk with a client and how a friendship or personal relationship should work. At home I try hard not to tell my friends and family about themselves. I seek to avoid "you" statements. As a therapist, however, part of my role is to say "you" often. A client is looking to me for a mirror of him or herself, so I say what I see. At home I would rather say, "I feel." At work I tend to say, "you feel."

The Choice to Return or Not

Near the end of the 50 minutes, I normally say, "I invite you to come back again. I am open to working with you, and I think coming here for a while might be helpful to you. Would you like to return?" Most people do, but some don't. When someone does want to return, I assume he or she has found some hope in my presence and feels that I can understand. People crave understanding. When someone doesn't want to return it's usually because he or she is still too scared of the process. My experience is that a client will schedule a second session even if he or she doesn't particularly like me, although they often cancel the second session the day before. It's hard for a client to tell a therapist, "I don't like you or trust you." In fact, when a client does tell the therapist that, usually the therapist's willingness to pay attention to that statement creates reconciliation that overcomes a bad first impression. But most clients are not strong enough to criticize a strange therapist.

There are some clients I don't want to work with. Almost always it's because I don't find them motivated to change or grow. They tend to be persons who blame others or are looking for a pill (and want to use me to get referred to a psychiatrist). I don't feel it's appropriate to say, "I don't want to work with you." That strikes me as using truth like a sledge hammer. Instead, I usually say, "I'm not sure you will find therapy helpful right now. Perhaps it would be best for you to consider some of what we've talked about and seek some focus and clarity about what kind of help you are seeking." Often such a client will later seek another therapist and tell that therapist that "Dr. McDonald told me I didn't need any help." I've had a lot a clients tell me about "stupid" therapists who shoved them out the door, saying they were hopeless. I usually don't buy it. What I assume is that the client wasn't ready for therapy before, or the therapist didn't want to work with him or her. It's usually not the therapist.

If the client wants to return, I usually say, "Then let's deal with practical matters."

Fee Negotiations

The biggest distinction between counseling and therapy is that counseling might be free, therapy has a fee involved. The reason a fee is important is not only because therapists have to eat, but most importantly it is because charging a fee allows the client to receive help without feeling obligation to the therapist. When I first started counseling, I did not charge a fee. At Christmastime all of my clients gave me presents. I sensed that their gifts was a kind of guilt offering, so I instituted a fee. They stopped giving me gifts. The fee freed them from an obligation to thank me.

Sometimes a client says to me, "I didn't know there'd be a fee." I simply say, "Yes, there is. I'm sorry I didn't make that clear to you on the front end. Does that affect whether or not you can or want to return?"

I tell them what my fee is, then ask, "Can you handle that?" If they indicate it will be difficult or impossible, I treat it like a negotiation: I have a "product" that I definitely consider worth my fee, but they might have extenuating circumstances that should merit further adjustment. If they can convince me to reduce it further, I will. If they can't convince me, I ask them to try paying the fee for a while and let me know if it's really the hardship they thought it would be. I add, "Our work together might be very important to you, something you need to invest something extra into."

Often I'm asked about insurance, to which I reply that as a pastoral counselor my counseling is usually not covered. Then I add, "Can you manage my fee if insurance won't help?" Some say yes; some say no. If they say no, I negotiate. I ask what their income and financial situation is and what they think they can afford. If they propose an amount that seems reasonable given their situation, I will lower my fee. If they are simply over-extended, I will say, "I understand that you are over-invested financially now, but therapy might be a very important investment for you to make. I'd like to stick with my fee for the time being and let you see if you can handle it. If you can't, let me know and we'll renegotiate. Are you willing to do that?"

Expectations and Future Appointments
After we've agreed upon the fee, I say, "I recommend you come weekly." I rarely recommend every other week. I don't find it to be as effective, for we spend too much

time "catching up," with less time available for serious investigation into problems or the self. I will see people every other week, but I usually discourage it.

We look at our schedules and seek a time to meet. I try to offer two or three options. I may have 10 options, but I've found that it's more helpful and efficient to offer two or three and let the client do some scheduling adjustment to take one of them. If he or she just can't, I offer a couple more options, until we find a convenient time. If we can't find a convenient time, I offer a time a couple or three weeks away. The usually reaction to that is to relent and change something so that we can meet next week, but sometimes we just have to postpone our next meeting.

I do not change my work or life schedule to accommodate a client. I will resent that, and my clients don't deserve my resentment.

I write down the appointment on my card and give it to them. This is on the back of my cards: "You have an appointment on _____ at_____ This time is reserved exclusively for you. 24 hours notice of cancellation is required or the fee will be charged." I point out the cancellation policy.

Although I am not presently distributing anything else, sometimes I have given clients a sheet explaining my "Guidelines and Understandings." What follows is the most literary and full description, which I have often used:

"What you share with me in the counseling context is held in confidence. No information will be given to a third party without your understanding and consent. The only exception to this policy would be in an extreme situation in which, in my judgment, there is a high risk of doing physical harm to self or others. In such an exceptional case, you will be informed.

"Any one hour session involves 50 minutes spent together. The remaining 10 minutes allow me time for making notes and responding to messages.

"The fee is to be paid at each appointment, unless otherwise arranged.

"At least 24 hours notice is required for cancellation or the fee will be charged.

"Every relationship has a beginning, a middle, and an end. Hence, if you decide to end your counseling, I ask that you plan on one full session as an ending.

At the Church Health Center we would give patients a brochure which includes the following information about pastoral counseling:

CHURCH HEALTH CENTER
PASTORAL COUNSELING & PSYCHIATRY GUIDELINES

The **purpose** of pastoral counseling is to offer help to individuals, couples, families, and children who are suffering from emotional, spiritual, behavioral, and relational problems at an affordable fee. Volunteer psychiatrists provide services for psychiatric problems at an affordable fee. We provide available medicines for Church Health Center medical patients at a small fee. (Medicines are not available to non-Church Health Center patients.)

We have two **expectations of patients**.

1. Patients are expected to pay at least a portion of their fee at each session, or pay at least **$2 a week**.

2. Patients are expected to pay for all appointments made with counselors and psychiatrists. The **fee will be**

charged for missed appointments or appointments that are canceled with less than a day's notice. This charge is added to your balance.

All contact with patients is kept strictly **confidential** within the professional confines of the Church Health Center.

Counseling sessions are **50 minutes** long, unless otherwise arranged. Psychiatric visits are 45 minutes for the initial interview, 30 minutes or less for subsequent visits. We try to begin and end on time.

All **appointments** are made through the pastoral counselors. Call 272-0003.

At each visit: we ask that you
1. **Check in** at front desk of the medical clinic building.
2. Receive your "superbill" and wait to be called.
3. Bring the "superbill" with you to the counseling office when called.
4. Return to the front desk of the medical clinic after the session with the completed superbill to pay your bill.

Thank you for your cooperation.

I used to hand out this form:

PASTORAL COUNSELING

What is pastoral counseling?

Pastoral counselors are ministers who specialize in counseling.

What kinds of problems do people bring to a pastoral counselor?

Depression, anxiety, marriage problems, problems with children, family problems. Most counseling is with individual adults, but often will include a spouse or family member.

Will anyone know I'm coming for counseling?

All of the Church Health Center services are kept confidential among the professional staff of the Center. We will not break that confidence without your consent.

What are the hours counseling is available?

Monday through Friday from 9:00 AM until 5:00 or 6:00 PM, and Monday and Thursday evenings until 9:00.

How much does it cost?

Our goal is to provide the best pastoral counseling at a cost you can afford. Our standard fee is $____ per session.

How can I make an appointment?

Call 272-0003 and ask for Dr. McDonald.

Finally, as we end the session, in my private practice I ask if I can touch base with the one who made the referral to thank him or her for the referral. Almost every client says yes, but some say no, which I honor without a simple "OK." The client usually tells me why, to which I reply, "That's all right with me. This will be between you and I only."

I usually say as I stand up to dismiss the client, "I'm glad you came, and I look forward to working with you. Have a good week."

I open the door and let the client out. Part of my ritual of letting go of the pain and hardship people share with me is that I control my own door. I open and close it to let them in, and I open and close it to let them out. It helps me shift back into my own life and let their lives be their own.

CHAPTER TEN
HOW TO REMEMBER

With people I counsel and connect well with I expect to remember their stories easily. I have found, however, that if I don't keep a few notes I forget some of the details that they expect me to remember. I do remember the feeling tone of initial sessions and a highlight or two from their lives, which I consider to be the most important thing to remember, but I forget a lot, often even when I'm absolutely sure I won't.

Why is it important to remember details? Two reasons: (1) it is a sign of respect, and (2) it is one of the most effective tools for building a good working alliance. Some clinicians focus an awful lot of attention to details and history, but I've found that such hard focus is usually a sign of that clinician's avoidance of transference/counter-transference experience. Remembering details and history are not the key to doing good therapy. Carefully seeking to remember some things, however, is a genuine expression of respect and will have a positive impact on the relationship.

Respect

When a client hands me his or her story, I am being given a sacred trust. I must keep that story safe and convey my deep respect for its importance. The simple statement, "I remember," is one of the most profound expressions of respect and reverence. The Biblical story is filled with injunctions to remember: remember when God took us out of the house of bondage in Egypt; remember that Jesus died for all of humanity; remember, remember. Remembering reminds us of who we are. Remembering reminds us of the importance of the relationship. When I remember what someone told me, I convey to that person that he or she is important to me. I trust that I will remember the experience of being with someone who shares openly with me as I pay close attention, and I will be able to convey that respect. To be able to remember all that was shared with me is beyond my ability and motivation. But I do want to be disciplined in my remembering. I need to write down some details and history to effectively jog my memory so that I can convey my respect for what was given to me.

Building a Working Alliance

In nearly every session I say, "I remember." Sometimes I refer to what happened in our session last week; sometimes to an event in a client's life; sometimes to a feeling of mine in the context of our relationship. Often a client is surprised that I can remember that. Some will even say, "You have a good memory." The truth is, though, that I do not have a particularly good memory unless I work at it. Part of the reason I seek to remember is because I do the work better when I do. When a client hears me remember accurately, there is an implicit invitation to share more openly, to trust more deeply, to be more real. Therapy works better under such circumstances.

It is just as important that I admit that I've forgotten some things, for the client needs to experience some level of frustration with this human relationship. All human relationships are frustrating, partly because in their self-centeredness our friends forget so much that we expected them to remember. Learning to live with this frustration without nursing it into anger and rage is part of what we all must achieve if we want to feel peacefully happy. So I don't try to remember everything. It's not only impossible; it's also not psychologically healthy. What I try to do is to remember well.

There are two types of information: factual and intuitive. Some therapists work best from a factual base and like to gather and sort detailed history to help in their understanding of the client. Others work best from an intuitive base and prefer only a little history and a lot of relational feel. They will base most of their work with the client on their relationship with the client. Both types of therapeutic styles certainly have my blessing. The two best therapists I know are opposites of one another on these matters. One is factual, the other is intuitive.

I am mostly intuitive, but I do prefer to have a few key facts. I do not like to gather these facts in a question-answer style. I prefer to gather them in the course of the conversation. However, were I to complete a thorough psychological examination of a client, what follows is what I'd include.

Seeking the Client's Core History

The first question I ask in the first session is "What's brings you here and how can I be of help?" Then I let the client talk. I prefer to let there be at least 15 minutes of conversation focused on the presenting problem and its immediate history. I follow the age-old adage of "Why here? Why now? Why me? How can I help?" At some appropriate point I'll interrupt to begin asking life history questions. I *never* ask everything I'm including here, but some do.

1. How old are you?
2. What is your relationship with your parents like?
3. Where are you in the family birth order?
4. Where were you raised?
5. What is your education and where did you receive it?
6. What kind of jobs have you had?
7. What was your childhood like?

8. What have your important intimate relationships been like?
9. What were the hardest years in your childhood?
10. What have been the hardest years in your adult life?

I also ask a question based upon my belief that early memories and early dreams are core metaphors:

11. What is your earliest memory?
12. Have you had a recurring dream?

Finally I ask a question that often presents their unconscious agenda for the therapy:

13. Did you have a dream last night?

Note Taking

I do not like to take written notes during a session, which therapists call "process notes", for four reasons. (1) If I spend 15 minutes immediately after the session doing a careful write-up, I'll remember what I need to know before the next session. (2) I want to convey to my clients that I will first and foremost treat them as a subject, not as an object. Taking process notes during the session signifies that the therapist is the objective clinician, not the friendly fellow traveler. (In some cases that's the best posture, but that's the exception, not the rule.) (3) The most alienating experience I ever had in my own personal therapy was with a therapist who wrote so much down of what I was saying in the first session that I felt his relationship was more with the paper than with me. I felt horribly discounted and vowed that I would seek to never do that to a client of mine. (4) Note taking follows a very obvious pattern that greatly influences the session. The therapist taking notes does so after certain kinds of statements and information, clearly implying what he or she is looking for, what is considered worthy of a note.

The client will invariably begin to emphasize things that he or she thinks the therapist considers important, somewhat determining the course of the session.

Diagnosis

Diagnosis comes from two root words, "*dia*," which means to divide, and "*gnosis*," which means to know. Diagnosis is the science of separating aspects of a client's problem in order to better understand what the problem is. The use of diagnostic terminology is one of the best ways to remember a client. There are two aspects of diagnosis: (1) the psychiatric diagnosis and (2) the dynamic diagnosis. The psychiatric diagnosis is the particular label we put on the problem or illness the client presents. It is the name of the problem. The dynamic diagnosis is the description of the problem using a combination of diagnostic categories. The psychiatric diagnosis is the name, the dynamic diagnosis is what we think we understand.

I use an intake form from the *Diagnosis and Statistical Manual IV* labeled as followed:

WORKING DIAGNOSES
AXIS I: CLINICAL SYNDROME & CODE:
AXIS II: PERSONALITY/DEVELOPMENTAL
           DISORDERS & CODE:
AXIS III: PHYSICAL DISORDERS/CONCERNS:
AXIS IV: PSYCHOSOCIAL STRESSORS
           (FAMILY/ECONOMIC/SOCIAL):

The Axis I diagnosis is the one the insurance companies want to know. This is the Major Depression, Dysthymic Disorder (which used to be Depressive Neurosis), Generalized Anxiety Disorder, etc.

I use Axis II mostly for my own shorthand. There is nothing more damning to a person than to give them a Personality Disorder label. To diagnose someone as Borderline, Narcissistic, or Dependent is like making a disclaimer that says, "I'm pretty sure this person is nearly incorrigible." The essential characteristic of a personality disorder is that their problems are grossly projected onto the outside world. In other words, a personality disordered person is one who says, "I don't have a problem. It's them!" Working with such a person is next to hopeless. For this reason, unless a patient is forcefully admitted to treatment, I tend to focus on the neurosis. A neurotic person admits that part of the problem is personal. If someone has come for personal help, then he or she cannot be stuck hopelessly in a personality disorder. Finally, the diagnosis of any personality disorder is often uninsurable. To file such a diagnosis for insurance coverage is usually asking for denial of the claim. Thus, I use Axis II as a shorthand for "personality style."

One of the most constructive educational projects I ever did in my clinical training was to carefully study the DSM to understand the personality disorders. I found in them a description of the basic personality styles:

1. <u>Paranoid</u> Style: "pervasive and unwarranted suspiciousness" that is expressed in a deep sense of mistrust and hypersensitivity.

2. <u>Schizoid</u> Style: extremely isolated self, loneliness covered over by apathy; a sort of hermit.

3. <u>Schizotypal</u> Style: odd, magical, mystical way of living with a less than fully grounded self; can be very likeable.

4. <u>Histrionic</u> Style: "overly dramatic, reactive, and intensely expressed behavior" that is often highly seductive or attractive in its passion and plea for

help; often seek compulsive partners to lean on, then criticize them for their coldness.

5. Narcissistic Style: grandiosity, self-importance, fantasies of unlimited success, and desire to be the center of attention to the point where there is a high degree of insensitivity to others; in a relationship the other person often feels like nothing; sometimes can be quite antisocial.

6. Antisocial Style: manipulative person with little conscience, a selfish chameleon; these are highly wounded and despairing people who often are either honorable among other thieves or somewhat avoidant in style too.

7. Borderline Style: instability, lives on the border of everything (good and bad relationships, job probation, craziness and sanity, etc.); most often associated with histrionics.

8. Avoidant Style: a very withdrawn person who does not particularly want to be isolated, but is mostly afraid of rejection and being shamed; the mild side of Schizoid.

9. Dependent Style: lack of self-confidence and tendency to lean passively onto others for help in most areas of life.

10. Compulsive Style: micro-manager of life, controlling with a cold edge, tends to be a workaholic, stingy, and appear emotionless; covers over an underlying dependency; often find histrionic and dependent persons to be in relation with—and then are highly critical of their irrationality.

11. Passive-Aggressive Style: highly self-defeating persons, habitually late or error-prone; tend to be sloppy, apologetic, and have lots of people mildly

annoyed at them; often associated with lots of depressed anger.

12. <u>Atypical, Mixed, or Other Style</u>: this is the catch-all category for the confused clinician. All persons are in fact mixed, unique, and comprised of some other stylistic characteristic that the above 11 names don't describe.

These eleven personality styles comprise the basis for my diagnostic impressions in Axis II. For me the most helpful of these is the histrionic label. The client who most often fools me is the histrionic one, so when I meet someone who seems histrionic I carefully talk myself into being objective, detached, and to not be blown around by the emotional winds.

Axis III has become much more important to me since I began working as the pastoral counselor for a medical clinic. I used to think that almost all physical problems are so deeply rooted in one's emotional coping that working on emotional issues is always in the foreground and physical issues are always in the background. Working around doctors and nurses, however, has made me much more aware of the interplay between the physical and the emotional and spiritual. It is simply true that anyone with back spasms that last over three days is going to get depressed. If those back problems last for three weeks, the person is going to wonder if he/she is capable of handling the problem. People with chronic physical ailments live on the border of emotional health. It's just not easy to feel good emotionally when you feel bad physically. So now I take physical concerns and issues very seriously. They are both an impacting factor and a key metaphor for usage in understanding and interpreting what's happening emotionally.

An example of the metaphorical quality of physical concerns is of a woman who wrenched her back at work, had months of physical therapy, got very depressed, and came to a therapist for help in coping with her depression. One of her biggest worries was new management that, although they still were inviting her back to work, was reorganizing the business. The therapist remarked, "These new managers are like back problems." Upon reflection she began to wonder if they were the cause of her back pain and the pain might not end until she resolved her conflicts with the new management. Her focus changed from her back to her work, relieving her of some of the stress that had kept her physical recovery in the slow lane.

Axis IV problems are present with any client. Family/ social/financial stressors are always a factor in the diagnosis. The DSM has some helpful categories for these issues in the "V Codes." Basically this is the descriptive area where I will write my perception of their complaints about others around them and my reflections about the core issues. For example, I might write, "Divorce with loneliness and grief; discouraged with having to start over. Unhappy about living with parents. Unstable finances. Guilt-ridden." Such a statement in many ways is the integration of Axis I, II, and III.

Essentially all people suffer from three basic problems: depression, anxiety, and relationship problems, and any diagnostic description needs to reflect a focus on one of these three problems.

In the DSM, the missing Axis is one's religious orientation, which has a powerful affect on treatment if the person is actively engaged in religious practice.

CHAPTER ELEVEN
THE CLIENT'S RELIGIOUS LIFE

I am very interested in what church, religion, or spiritual orientation a person has. The religious orientation of a client is routinely the most discounted factor in the diagnosis and understanding of what makes the person tick. It is also up there in importance with the physical, emotional, and social. Any sound diagnosis of any problem should be dissected into fours. It is no accident that the mandala shows up so often. The world, our worlds, operate in fours:

- God, Christ, the Holy Spirit, and the Demonic;
- relationship with God; for the serenity to change what you can, to accept what you can't change, and the wisdom to know the difference;
- physical, emotional, social, and religious.

The religious drive parallels and compliments the basic psychological question, "What does that mean?", with the basic theological question: What does life mean?" Psychology asks about particular experiences, dreams, relationships. Theology asks about universal experiences. Eknath Easwaran (1994) writes about "the questions that matter most: Who am I? What is the nature of the human being? Is there a purpose to life? How can I live at my highest? And, finally, what happens when I die?" Anytime we discount these questions, we reduce human life and problems to a more trivial level.

A person's worship life is the key to their struggle to answer these questions. That worship life might be very formal or quite accidental. Some people claim to find more meaning in rock climbing than in attending church services. When I meet such a person I seek to understand how his or her experience in rock climbing embraces these key questions.

The basic religious questions that I seek to look for in counseling are these:

- How is this person seeking a happier life, that is, seeking to find "life more abundant"?
- How does this person understand his or her purpose in life?
- Where does this person experience moments of grace or acceptance?
- How does this person pray?

Let me explain the roots of these questions.

Life More Abundant

Deep inside of each of us is a hope that life can be consistently great. We all experience moments of bliss and peace, but we get discouraged because these moments are fleeting. We also are envious of those persons who appear to enjoy life everyday, despite its problems and suffering. What is it that makes some people so consistently happy and others so moody? I have found that everyone has a more or less articulated theory of how to achieve and sustain happiness. We can answer the question of what would make me happy. Not without doubt, but with some degree of self-assurance.

I often use a simple metaphor to help me understand a client's personal view of what he or she is looking for as well as to encourage looking at this issue. I talk about "depression," a mood we all experience. We are all traveling on a journey where there are many ruts, or depressions. Each time we come to these depressions we are tempted to find ways over them—medications, tricks, rigid religion—any way that would be easier than going through the depression.

I believe that at the bottom of these depressions is a treasure, and if we have the guts to slide down into the hole, and if we have the strength to muck around at the bottom, we'll find the treasure. And if we still have the energy to pull that treasure out the other side, as we continue on our journeys, we'll now have something of great value. The purpose of this metaphorical image is to encourage clients to choose the hard way, which is the religious way, or, as Christians call it, "the way of the cross." It is also to introduce them to the idea that therapy is most importantly symptom relief. Most importantly, therapy is a search for truth and treasures. The therapeutic journey that includes the religious quest is not easy.

Why shouldn't it be easy? one might ask. The reason is because wisdom comes through suffering. We might gain knowledge from disciplined, structured work or study, but it is in going through our suffering, sliding down into the depression, where wisdom is born.

Purpose in Life

The great question of theology is "What does life mean?" Or stated differently, "What is the purpose of life?" There are two ways we respond to this question. One is vocational, the other is our worldview. Vocationally we must feel that there is some reason other than toil for our life's work. We may be in a job that we don't like now, but it is tolerable if we believe it is leading in a direction that will eventually get us where we want to go. If we don't feel we're going in the right direction vocationally, we're not going to be feeling very good. Right there is the core problem for many clients, and the work of therapy follows the course of helping them change their vocational direction.

Our worldview is our root understanding of why the world operates the way it does. In the wild some say survival is the focus of all life. Humans, in creating basically secure environments, have created much more complicated worldviews. Albert Schweitzer proposed "reverence for life." Immanuel Kant proposed a search for dignity. Martin Luther King, Jr., offered "the search for the beloved community." Less renowned persons often suggest, "to love and care for my family;" "to be a good person;" "to make the world better for my children." One of the purposes of therapy is to help each person articulate his or her own worldview, for when one's vision is clear, the path to it is easier to follow. In other words, we feel good when we're doing what is right, and what is right must be in line with our understood worldview.

Experiencing Grace or Acceptance

Every person I've known has deep within their soul a belief that "if someone would know me most deeply and accept me fully, he or she would find me very good and loveable." (They also feel just the opposite at times.) Even the people with the worst self-images have this belief. It's as if there's some song way down inside that might get very quiet, but it won't stop singing completely. Perhaps one who commits a despairing suicide can't hear the singing, but even with those persons, I think they've lost hope of ever finding such a healing person who would affirm their goodness. (Besides, I think suicide is basically more of an angry, aggressive act than one of total despair—for suicide sure does mess up the lives of others.)

Grace is experienced through openness. It is experienced most often in being open with another person. I want to know if a client has a confidant with whom he or she sometimes experiences grace. If so, I want us to amplify that experience, both in the therapeutic relationship (that is, I want therapy to build on the best of that relationship), and in their relationships with others beyond the confidant. The grace-filled life is one characterized most simply by the healthy transactional analysis position: "I'm OK; you're OK." It is definitely much easier to live life with acceptance than critically.

Prayer

Finally, I want to know how a client expresses his or her deepest yearnings and sense of praise. I don't usually ask, "How do you pray?" That is experienced by many as an intrusive religious question. For some it's not, but I find there are better ways to learn the answer to this question. Most importantly, the answer is inherent in the therapeutic hour. Therapy done carefully is a prayer in itself. Therapy should help a person express one's deepest yearning, and each session should end with some sense of thankfulness. Even the sessions ending in anxiety and pain should include some sense of the importance of the material talked about, some sense of rightness about the process. Certainly not every session does, but it needs to. Clients who often leave the therapeutic hour with lots of ambivalence eventually figure out that the therapy is not working well and either drop out of therapy or seek another therapist.

CHAPTER TWELVE
FAMILY DYNAMICS

No diagnosis is complete without an assessment of the family surrounding the client. Over the years I've come to see that there is one basic family issue: the family's level of enmeshment or differentiation. I measure this with three measuring sticks: (1) the degree to which I hear the word "you"; (2) triangulaion; and (3) quality of leadership.

"You-ing" One Another

An enmeshed family is a family where the problem of any member of the family is a problem for everyone. So because in a family there's always someone with a problem at any given time, in an enmeshed family, everyone always has a problem. Enmeshed families are made up of problem people. It's as if everyone in the family needs the others to be over-involved in their lives. There just isn't room for individuation. What an enmeshed family can't stand is "I." So the primary pronoun is "you." We can measure the level of enmeshment of a family simply by listening to how they talk about the others, that is, how much they say "you." Enmeshed families "You" each other to death: "You did this to me;" "You've got to stop that;" "You make me feel . . . ;" "You are the problem."

The opposite of the enmeshed family is the family made up of differentiated members. Their primary word is "I": "I feel this way;" "I like that;" "I want to do this;" "I want things to be different;" "I will do this;" "I will not tolerate that." Such a family will still have problems, but because a single problem is not everyone's problem, problems are magnified and attempts at solving them are not contaminated.

Midway between "you" and "I" is "we." Families that use "we" in describing their problems are sometimes scared to let an individual find his or her own way; sometimes appropriately owning the communal nature of the problem. A therapist has to make a judgment on the appropriateness of the "we" based upon intuition.

Families that are more often than not functional, healthy, and happy, are more differentiated than enmeshed. The family therapist's job is to encourage differentiation.

I will address this much more thoroughly in Part II.

Triangulation is Strangulation

Family studies have helped us realize that enmeshment functions in threes, that is, in triangles. When two persons are interacting, there are two things happening: (1) me to you an (2) you to me. Simple. But as soon as a third party (or issue) enters the dyad, suddenly there's also (3) me to it, (4) it to me, (5) you to it, (6) it to you, (7) you and me to it, (8) you and it to me, (9) it and me to you; and (10) all of us together. Five times as much is happening! That's like being on a merry-go-round that is going too fast. You can't let go, or you'll fall off and get hurt. If you stay on, you'll get dizzy or sick. You can't see well; you can't dance. You're just paralyzed. That's just what triangulation does.

Families that are dysfunctional are triangulated. Thus a therapeutic endeavor is to de-triangle members of the family. Problems can be solved between twos, but not between threes.

Triangles are also how games work. Games are the ways that families interact to get to familiar bad places. In a game there's always (1) a persecutor, (2) a victim, and (3) a rescuer. Every time I see triangles I know that people are not only paralyzed and confused, but the family games have control, not the people and their better judgment.

Leadership

There are two key qualities to look for in the leadership strengths/weaknesses of a family. One is the degree of self-differentiation among family members. Differentiation is not just the opposite of enmeshment, but more importantly the degree to which a person can stand solid when a family or work system is shaking in its anxiety. Anxiety is normal in a family or system, for we all must cope with pending death, questions of meaning, and knowledge of guilt, but the differentiated person is one who is not swallowed up by system anxiety. He or she is able to maintain a clear sense of selfhood that is calm, not anxiety driven.

The second quality of leadership is vision. Is there a person in the family who has a vision of health and an idea of how to get there? Or is the family mired in despair, wishing for respite without any idea how to get there or what exactly it would look like?

CHAPTER THIRTEEN
RIGHT AFTER THE SESSION

As soon as possible after the first session I do a careful write-up using the following format.

CHURCH HEALTH CENTER
Pastoral Counseling Intake
Client:

CLIENT INFORMATION:

Age:
Sex:
Ethnic Background:
Job:
Salary:
Marital Status:
Children:
Fee:

PRESENTING PROBLEM AND CURRENT HISTORY
OF PROBLEM:

DESCRIPTION OF CLIENT (AS A JAM MOSAIC)—
Appearance:
Speech:
Affect:
Judgment:
Attitude:
Mood:
Memory:
Orientation:
Sensorium:
Abstraction:
Intelligence:
Content of session:

HISTORY/FORMULATION/GENOGRAM:

RELIGIOUS AFFILIATION:

THEOLOGICAL DIAGNOSIS:
(include stage of faith—held, story, group, questioning, owned, universal; awareness of the Holy; sense of hope/trust vs. despair/mistrust; experience of grace vs. judgment; sense of calling vs. confusion of purpose; openness vs. isolation):

WORKING DIAGNOSES (DSM IV)

AXIS I: CLINICAL DISORDERS & OTHER CONDITIONS THAT MAY BE A FOCUS OF CLINICAL ATTENTION:

AXIS II: PERSONALITY/
DEVELOPMENTAL DISORDERS:

AXIS III: GENERAL MEDICAL CONDITIONS/
CONCERNS:

AXIS IV: PSYCHOSOCIAL & ENVIRONMENTAL PROBLEMS: (FAMILY/ECONOMIC/SOCIAL):
- Problems with primary support group:
- Problems related to social environment:
- Educational problems:
- Occupational problems:
- Housing problems:
- Economic problems:
- Problems with access to health care services:
- Problems related to interaction with legal system/crime:
- Other psychosocial and environmental problems:

AXIS V: GLOBAL ASSESSMENT OF FUNCTIONING
SCALE:

RECOMMENDATIONS, TREATMENT PLAN, AND
GOALS:

Signature and Date of Interview:

This takes me about 10-15 minutes now, but early in my work I would spend a half-hour at least on each write-up, partly because I wasn't sure what was essential for me to remember, partly because I knew my supervisors would read what I wrote and I needed to gain their confidence. Now I have a better idea of what is essential for my memory and what other clinicians might like to know should they take over my work with the client. I still write to gain or maintain the confidence of my peers. Doctors at my clinic have access to my notes, so I want them to have confidence in my assessment.

At the Church Health Center I have been introduced to a structure for note-taking that I now use after each session. We use the letters S.O.A.P. to represent:

S = Subject matter discussed

O = Objective thoughts on the client

A = Assessment or diagnosis

P = Plan of treatment.

For example, I might write:

S—talked of conflict with mother; related it to problems at home when she was 13; plans to talk with her next month when she goes home.

O—this may have a major impact on her frustrations in the marriage.

A—Depression; development arrested in early teens

P—see next week; help her plan how to talk effectively with mother.

Legal Issues

Clients have a legal right to obtain my notes. Lawyers have a legal write to supeona them. Thus, I don't write damning information in my notes. I also don't write judgmental information in them, like referring to a session as boring or the client as a jerk. I realize that writing down a diagnosis is a way of objectifying the client and might be painful to read, but it is a compromise I make in negotiating through the narcissistic world of professionalism. We professionals think it is our gift to be able to diagnosis properly, but it is really our sin. It is a sin I have to commit. If I didn't use the diagnostic nomenclature, my professional colleagues wouldn't respect me as much and I'd have a tougher time making a living. It does help our work, but it can hurt, too.

I have a policy when clients request my notes. I do not authorize our clinic secretaries to disseminate any counseling notes until after I have spoken with the client making the request. What I say is this:

"Although you have a right to your records, because we write our notes in clinical language it often appears that we were looking at you as a object, not as the real person we counseled with. You may have your records if you wish, but I am concerned that if you read something that seems confusing or stirs up feelings that you call me so I can seek to clarify things."

I don't really like giving out my notes, because I consider them an intrusion into an I-Thou relationship (turning it into I-it). But the law says I have to. What I try to do is to lessen the possible alienating impact by this policy.

Contacting the Referral Source

Sometimes it is helpful to get information from a referral source. I don't consider it essential, however, because I consider my job primarily to be contained in the counseling hour. If a client tells me a pack of lies, I might be able to discover the truth by contacting the referral source, but I take the position that if a client is lying, he or she needs to lie for some reason, and I will discover in the appropriate time and appropriate way the reasons for the lies. The truth will be revealed in the relationship.

However, most clients don't mind me contacting the referral source, for they prefer that I take some shortcuts to understanding.

I contact referral sources in two ways. First, I contact them to thank them for the referral and simply let them know that I will or will not be continuing to work with the client. Second, I sometimes ask for their records. In the latter case I need written permission from the client. I use a very simple form.

RELEASE OF RECORDS FORM

I [client's name] authorize the release of all records and information from [therapist's name and address] pertaining to my treatment to Dr. Ron McDonald [my address].

This release will be valid for one year from this date.

_____

signed date

I seek records mostly for children, although if an adult client has had extensive therapy somewhere else, it often eases the transition for me to have read those records.

CHAPTER FOURTEEN
THE SECOND SESSION

The second session is usually the most awkward session. The initial goal of assessment and recommendations that was so obvious in the first session will now give way to the work of psychotherapy, which is difficult to define. *I define psychotherapy as the intentional reflection on life experience in the context of a confidential relationship.* The difference between counseling and psychotherapy is the depth of that reflection. In counseling we tend to look at problems. In therapy we look also at unconscious matters. In counseling we look for solutions. In therapy we also seek to illuminate what has been hidden. The reason why I prefer to work as a therapist, not just a counselor, is because I believe that there is a huge percentage of ourselves kept in darkness. The larger that percentage is the more likely we are to mug ourselves, contributing mightily to the problems we want to get away from. Counseling that focuses on helping us get away from those problems barely touches the ways we help set ourselves up. Therapy's purpose is to help us live more in the light, reducing the percentage of ourselves living in darkness.

The opening of the second session will go a long ways towards inviting the client to see the therapeutic relationship as counseling or as psychotherapy. Consider the different between opening the second session with, "What problem do you want to focus on today?", and "What would you like to talk about?" The former question is easier, but limiting. The latter is harder, but more open. As I wrote earlier, the best therapy is founded on openness, on faith. Eventually, good therapy does not even need the therapist to open a session in any way other than to open the door to his or her office, be quiet, and let the client begin. My best work is done with silence being my best therapeutic tool. The opening of the second session should let the client know that the time is yours, I will give you plenty of space. I have no particular agenda. You may set your own agenda.

I have one exception to this position. If there is an issue related to the frame of the therapy, I bring that to our attention at the start of the session. I want to get my agenda out of the way as quickly as possible. For example, if I heard some crucial information about the client from an outside source, I might open the session by saying, "In speaking with your doctor last week, he told me that you have been seriously ill a couple of times during the last year." That would probably be all I would say, conveying to the client that I have some information about you that you didn't tell me, and I don't keep such information secret from you. I want the client to know that what I know about him or her is what he or she knows that I know, nothing more. If, however, the doctor simply spoke well of the client, I might decide the recommendation is innocuous enough to not need to bring up and interrupt the flow of the session. I might share the recommendation. I'm not 100% consistent on this matter, except when the information is obviously very important. Then I don't keep secrets.

Phone Calls From the Family

Every therapist occasionally gets a call from a friend or family member of the client who says, "Let me tell you about [your client], but you mustn't tell." I used to reassure the caller that I would keep the ensuing information in confidence. I quickly found out that I had accepted a role of secret-keeper from the very person I was seeking to help open up. It's not good position for the therapist to be in.

In accepting such information in confidence I unwittingly undermined the integrity of the therapeutic relationship. I've solved that problem by saying from the outset of the phone conversation: "I don't accept information about my client unless I am free to share the information and its source with my client. If you wish to tell me anything about my client I must be free to convey your concern with the client." With that said, the information is not a secret I have to keep. The caller quickly knows that I honor the therapeutic relationship first and foremost and will not collect secret data. In my experience, such a position usually does not shut up the caller, but the conversation quickly stops the attempted conspiracy. And I know I sure feel better! Therapy doesn't work too well when the therapist is a co-conspirator against the client.

Preparation

Just prior to the second session it is important to do two things: review the intake notes, and center-in. It is not respectful or good work to enter a session with scattered thoughts about a new client. It is a reasonable expectation of the client that the therapist will recall important matters from the first session. No matter how much I trust my memory, if I don't check my notes and jog my memory of the client and the first session, I will not be fully prepared for the second session. This is all the more true for the therapist with a large case-load.

Jogging the memory is an important element in centering-in. The second element in centering is to remind myself of my emotional reaction to the client. I need to remember how I felt and reflect on why I felt that way. This puts me back in touch with the human side of the new relationship.

Centering also includes reminding myself of the sacred ground we came to. I remind myself that this client is a child of God and in some way is seeking restoration of the soul. My job is sacred.

Gratitude and Idealization

A good first session inevitably causes the client to be very grateful to the therapist. Such a beginning serves two primary spiritual purposes: (1) it gives the client a good dose of hope, and (2) it allows the therapist to be idealized. Theologically it allows the client to recreate a savior-figure. I've always found it difficult to accept such projections. I know myself well enough to know that I'm not a savior. It's kind of like having someone praise me too much. I want to protest, "No, I'm not that good." Of course, another part of me relishes such praise. Any therapist is capable of enjoying being worshipped. But that's what makes us not worthy of being worshipped.

The joy of being a therapist, however, depends to some degree on our willingness to accept the client's projections without protest. We have to trust that patiently reflecting reality back to the client—what is real instead of what is idealized—will give him or her the freedom and courage to accept oneself and find one's own true savior. Instead of responding by discounting the idealization, I try to respond in a more factual or mirroring way: "So you see me as more helpful than others you have gone to." The client might be even more complimentary: "Not just 'more helpful', you are the *best* I've ever been to." To such a comment I might say, "I'm glad I've been so helpful."

Part of what makes it disconcerting to be idealized is what I call "the pedestal dilemma." The top of a pedestal is an exhilarating place to be (assuming one is not afraid of heights!), but it's also easy to fall off of. To stand on top of a pedestal takes good balance and substantial calm. One can't get too excited or nervous. Here is another reason why a therapist must be a well-grounded, well-balanced person. By the second session, most clients pressure therapists to buy into the notion that we are better than we really are. Within one hour the therapist is being worshipped in a way that is a highly seductive call to grandiosity. Theologically we call this the temptation to blasphemy. That's a serious offense! Blasphemy is, of course, pretending to be God or equal to God. That's what got the people at Babel in trouble, and that's what the client has just told us we seem like, and it's awful easy to enjoy the sin.

It is crucial that the therapist receive the projection without accepting its assertion. Therapists must remember that we are human, not gods, and that if there is a savior at work, that divinity is flowing through the therapist in spite of our faults. Our job is to be as open as possible so that divine grace and hope might not be blocked from reaching the client who so desperately needs help out of despair.

The Therapist's Desires with Very Attractive Clients

Many clients are very interesting and attractive persons. It is normal for a therapist to feel a friendly attraction to such persons, wanting to be considered a friend. One of the difficulties of being a therapist is accepting the need to be friendly but not a friend. Friends share their mutual needs with one another. A therapist's job is to provide a friendly atmosphere for the client that is unencumbered by the therapist's need for friendship. Very often I will meet a client who is so much like me—someone I would love to have as my friend—that I have to remind myself of my role as therapist. Therapists simply cannot be friends with their clients. Yes, we are friendly, but we are not friends. We have to choose.

A second type of desire the therapist has with a client is sexual. Some clients are very sexy to the therapist. It is difficult to not engage in the fantasy of becoming impressive and sexually attractive to the client. Again, though, the therapist must be reminded that the job of therapist is not a normal relationship. It is a sacred trust. Our job is to be there for the client, not to get our own needs met (except financial). Sometimes just reminding ourselves of this, however, doesn't quell our desires. At such times we must admit our need for help. It is imperative that a therapist get supervisory or therapeutic help when desires for a client get overwhelming. It is absolutely wrong to engage in a sexual relationship at any level with a client, for it profanes sacred ground. Sex and sexual provocations from the therapist are in the "forbidden zone."

Therapy takes place on three levels. On the behavioral level, we look at how problems are acted out and seek practical solutions. On an emotional level we look at reactions to events and troubles and seek to release the client from depressed or out of control feelings. On a sacred level, we look at the deepest levels of meaning and trust in the soul. At this level we need to, like Moses at the burning bush, take off our shoes, for we are on holy ground. Whenever sex at any level happens between therapist and client, we defile this holy ground. The wound it creates is very deep. It is wrong.

Desires, however, are normal. It is even normal to have sexual fantasies regarding a client, but they must be tempered with the remembrance of our role. We must remind ourselves that a fantasy is a fantasy—and that's

OK—but leave it as a fantasy. It is not to be shared or in any way acted out. If we get tempted to either share the fantasy or act it out, we must get help!

The first time I spoke with a supervisor about a very strong sexual attraction to a client, I was worried about my own lust. I did trust my ability to control my behavior, but was concerned that my lust would contaminate my perceptions and interpretations. I was trying hard to not lust for her. Try as I might, I could not quell my feelings and fantasies. My supervisor asked me, "Are you afraid you are going to act out these feelings?" I replied that I wasn't, and, after discussing my behavioral restraints and my understanding of the ethics involved, my supervisor, who was female, said, "Sometimes it's nice to be in the presence of someone so sexy, isn't it?" I smiled and said, "Yes, it's great!" suddenly aware that I could actually enjoy my sexual feelings—maybe even without them bothering me. From that moment on I have acknowledged that although a therapist may not be a sexual participant with a client, a therapist is a sexual person who can enjoy sexual feelings, keep them from the client, and still be open to client's emotional needs. I am, however, very clear that I will not be a sexual participant in a client life.

Male therapists have an additional issue to consider. We may not be as casual about touching and hugging clients as female therapists might be. I know some women therapists who use touch as part of their therapeutic technique, but men just cannot do that. Masculine sexuality is such that touch from a male therapist is overloaded with confusing messages. For one, there is a terrible history of men as abusers and rapists, and people in our culture are keenly aware of that history. Too many men have simply not had good sexual ethics, and probably half of the women we see in therapy have been the victims of such men. To touch these women is often going to be experienced as intrusive or sexual, not mere affection. Secondly, whereas female sexuality is more receptive and nurturing by nature, masculine sexuality is more probing and protective. Therapy by men needs to be a gentle holding, and touch is often overloaded with the thrusting nature of sex for men. Plus, despite the great need to protect that men can offer, that very dynamic can easily be experienced by many women as being overwhelmed.

With all that said, I still do touch my clients, male and female, in two ways. First, I am willing to shake hands as someone enters or touch someone on the back as he or she exits my office. I do not, however, rub someone's back. I touch gently, conveying affection. I am careful to not pull the person to me, as well as to not push him or her out the door. I do not touch someone new, but only someone with whom I feel genuine affection. It is a father's type of touch, and I pay close attention to the client's reaction. If I sense a strong response, we talk about it the next week. I will say, "When I touched you as you left last week, I notice that you reacted [in a particular manner]. What happened to you?" Secondly, I will hug sometimes a client if the client asks for a hug. I do it with care and carefulness. My guiding principle is "affection is OK, sexual expressions are not." If I sense the request for a hug is a sexual request, I refuse it and suggest that we talk about the request. I will say, "I want to understand what feelings or desires you have behind that request." I often will add, "It is not that the request is wrong, or that your feelings or desires are wrong. It is that this relationship is too important for us to ignore what you are truly experiencing." Sometimes I have to remind the client that the therapeutic relationship is friendly, but not a friendship, warm and affectionate, but not to be sexual.

We must be careful about sexuality in therapy, for it is a powerful force, the focus of much need, much abuse, and much fun.

History Structure

A central element of the second session is the need to fill in some blanks in the therapist's understanding of the client's history. The therapist should not assume he or she knows enough of the client's story. It is very appropriate to ask many questions about details and omitted facts.

In doing so the therapist will be able to point out common themes in the client's many stories. Sharing these musings are an important part of the second session. They give the client a deeper sense of the value of sharing. Having a second person analyze one person's experience can be highly enriching. One purpose of the second session is to sell the client on continuing this valuable process, and pointing out historical patterns is a great way to demonstrate the value of insight. When we understand ourselves better, something inside of us resonates with such relief that we feel a sudden surge of power over our own lives. It is the experience of grace—the gift of life and the freedom to live it unencumbered by ignorance.

PART III
THE STAGES OF CHANGE IN THE THERAPEUTIC PROCESS

In the late 1980s I interviewed about a dozen people who felt that their experience in psychotherapy had radically changed their lives. I asked them particularly about their experience in therapy and why they thought it was important. Gradually, as the interviews unfolded I began to see common patterns and themes. They described four stages of change they went through in their therapeutic journeys. What consistently happened to these people was, initially, an experience of changing from a position of *shame* that had for some time kept them from seeking help to a position of *humility* when they finally sought help. There may be a fine line between humiliation and humility, but it is not a small change, for shame thwarts change while humility is a prerequisite for change. Shame paralyzes; humility is a virtue.

Secondly, people entering therapy found an immediately different perspective on their problem. Instead of maintaining a defensive, closed posture, they were encouraged to open up, and that openness truly changed their lives. Openness is a radically different way of living from our normally anxious, defensive, and belief-oriented way of life. As I explain this further, I will assert that this is the true posture of faith.

Thirdly, people reported to me that therapy encouraged them to approach their important relationships in a new way, what we call differentiation. They became less reactive and combative in those relationships, and therefore able to transform them, sometimes radically, sometimes just slightly—but normally with more peace.

This peacefulness was reported to be a factor in their fourth change. These people found a deeper spiritual life. This wasn't just a return to religious beliefs or activities of their past. Some reported turning further away from those structures. It was an experience of a deepening curiosity with religious or spiritual matters. Indeed, for most it was accompanied by joining a religious community, but the most striking aspect of this change was that the introspective tendency that had been part of earlier changes now included a sense of mystery or transcendence. Furthermore, it always was received with gratitude. Thankfulness appears to be a part of this change.

Those were the changes I could identify from listening to these folks, and they are the changes expounded upon in the following chapters.

CHAPTER FOURTEEN
THE TRANSFORMATION OF HUMILITY

People in trouble experience great embarrassment. They are ashamed of their troubles, especially men are. In this state of humiliation, many people will not call for help. They think they should be able to take care of their own problems. Unable to take care of themselves like they think that ought to, paralyzed in shame, they refuse to seek help, even as matters get worse.

Humiliation is an extreme sense of shame. Shame is the common emotion we feel when we mess up, feeling "no good." Unlike guilt, which is judging our behavior as inadequate or inappropriate, shame attacks our sense of self. Guilt is primarily a thought process. Shame is an emotional attack on ourselves. Humiliation is the sense of total failure. To feel humiliated is to feel totally ashamed of oneself. It is a hollow, empty feeling. It paralyzes us, hits us in the gut, and saps us of energy. When humiliated we always feel alone and very lonely. Because shame is so isolating and lonely, it is tough to seek any kind of help when in this state. Those who are unable to move beyond humiliation will develop a deep sense of unworthiness, which is usually covered over by a refusal to admit any faults. Unable to cope with their own attacks on themselves, these people often protect themselves with judgmentalness and condescension.

Into this isolated and dark place of humiliation is a seemingly slight but momentous change: the small but dramatic step from humiliation to humility. A person who finally confesses to a therapist a desire to change, an admission of despair, or a confession of guilt is prepared to experience the healing, liberating quality of humbleness. When we approach another person confessing our shortcomings and separation from health and happiness, we are embracing this first stage of healing change—humbleness. Confession is the key to humility.

Humility, however, is not the same as self-effacement. Even though humbleness has historically often been understood as poverty, the humility that changes a person becomes a source of wealth. That is why Jesus could assert that the humble or the meek would inherit the earth. There may be nothing as liberating as the realization that we are accepted, that we have no more need for defensiveness. Paul Tillich (1955) calls it the greatest experience that we can have. And he is right. Humility is always accompanied by grace, and is therefore the foundation for the inward peacefulness so yearned for.

This kind of humility includes a sense of pride that is different from the sin of pride. As the Church teaches, the sin of pride is the attitude that sets oneself apart from humanity, the attitude of the person who refuses to admit fault. But there is a different kind of pride—pride in the creation of beauty, pride in the watching of a loved one grow. Such pride motivates one to participate in the magnificent creativity that is part of the human story. Have you not felt the great surge of humility that accompanies the reading of a great book, or the seeing of a beautiful piece of art? A strange thing this is, for the experience of beauty makes us feel proud and happy to be alive while simultaneously elicits the commonality that is part of humility. This is the feeling of awe, the emotion which unifies pride and humility in its most constructive and powerful manner.

But humility is so close to shame. Beauty can elicit awe, or one might react with shame, "I couldn't have done that; I'm not very talented." Sometimes when we err, we are so blatantly wrong, it's extremely difficult to forgive ourselves. We might even be able to admit the mistakes, but deep inside are horrified at ourselves: "How could I do that?" Shame is just an inch away from a comparison with someone else who has done well, and it's just an inch away from our next major mistake.

Shame is often so debilitating that one cannot see the potential for healing that accompanies humility. It is a horrible feeling to be ashamed of oneself. We avoid it by all sorts of means, usually by blaming and denying fault. The reason we do this is because it is not easy to develop a self-image that is strong enough to not need constant defense, a self-image that can stand confession. Avoiding shame feels necessary. What in fact is really necessary, however, is a way to rise above shame, not a way to avoid it. A helpful way to do this is to develop a posture of undefendedness.

Undefendedness

"Undefendedness" is a concept used by a pastoral counselor friend of mine, Jack Wortman. It is that state of being when one is able to confessionally face the deepest levels of human frailty while still feeling at peace with oneself, not needing to defend oneself from attack. It is the state of genuine self-acceptance, not of arrogance and self-exaltation, but of living graciously with oneself. It is a posture of faith, of opening up, that is based on the trust that grace will abide, that love and hope are eternal and ever present. It is a simple posture, but difficult to maintain, for it depends on relentlessly continuing on the path of becoming less defended against those inner conflicts which restrict us. It calls us to get behind the defenses and re-experience our personality restrictions to be freed from early wounds and decisions. There is no easy or swift way to do this.

We are introduced to undefendedness by being in the presence of someone who is undefended. In the presence of such a mentor we experience acceptance and safety that allows us to muster up the courage to face ourselves. An undefended person is one who is not afraid, not even afraid of another's aggression. One senses that the undefended person can be hurt, but embraces hurt, claiming ownership of his/her own emotions no matter what they are. S/he can be changed and will likewise own those changes. In his/her presence one feels a sense of emotional logic that says, "If this person I am with is able to remain undefended in spite of the threats I perceive, then what I am defending myself against must not be so dangerous." Undefendedness begets undefendedness. There is a quiet confidence that transforms the surrounding environment much like Daniel in the lion's den, or Shadrak, Meshack, and Abendego in the fiery furnace. It is easy to look at Jesus as this type of person.

The undefended person embraces a capacity for suffering that transforms sacrifice into resurrection. Joseph Campbell (1988) writes, "The one who suffers is, as it were, the Christ, come before us to evoke the one thing that turns the human beast of prey into a valid human being. That one thing is compassion." Because the undefended person is willing to withstand the attack and ridicule of others, we find ourselves feeling compassion for him or her. The willingness to suffer is disarming and magnetic.

When an undefended person walks into a conflict, whether it be a marital conflict, a job struggle, or a political battle, his/her presence will take down the sails of defensiveness. The undefended person has peacemaking power that leaves the potential antagonist with the distinct impression that owning one's errors will not result in humiliation. He or she seems to feel not only no need to defend, but also no need to attack. For in fact, the undefended person is one filled with humility and thus fully in touch with his or her commonality with humanity. In such a presence, instead of feeling afraid to confess, we feel more at easy with confession. And we are surprised to find that confession facilitates the calm of humility.

To be a competent psychotherapist one must aspire to undefendedness. That is certainly a daunting task, but one that the Work of psychotherapy demands. This is another reason why psychotherapist must experience the humble work of being in their own psychotherapy, and it is the best argument for why continuing supervision throughout one's career is highly advisable. The competent psychotherapist must be humble, for humility is the first stage of change in spiritual growth.

CHAPTER FIFTEEN
THE TRANSFORMATION OF FAITH

The word "faith" is commonly used as synonymous with "belief". My faith" is "my belief." Faith, however, is virtually the opposite of belief. Beliefs are important, even crucial in our lives. They are our security blankets, defining our sense of right and wrong, justice and injustice, good and bad, divine and demonic. Beliefs are necessary for our daily sense of security. Because I believe this and that, I am not normally anxious. Beliefs help us relax. Beliefs are the house we live in. They give us safe boundaries; keep us safely within a box. Some people have highly restrictive beliefs and thus live in a tight box. Other people have quite liberal beliefs and enjoy great freedom within a larger box. To live with beliefs is to live within the confines of a box, but it can be a very big or very small box. Beliefs are like the frame around a picture. They help define our lives.

Faith, however, is very different from belief. Faith in the Biblical Pauline sense is more akin to openness. Fundamentally, faith means openness and radical trust. Openness is the opposite of belief. Certainly liberal beliefs can give one much room to live, but living based upon beliefs, no matter how liberal, is still living in a box. Openness has no walls, no frame. Faith that means openness means living so radically that beliefs no longer matter. Were it not for the correlated characteristic of radical trust, faith as mere openness would be frightening. Faith, though, is based on a deep abiding trust that one can be radically open to life-itself.

In Paul's writings, especially in Galatians and Romans, the paradox of faith is that with it there is no need for law; because of faith, there is no desire to break the law, hence, no need for laws. It is this paradox that Augustine understood when he suggested we "love God and do what you want." To love God, the act of faith itself, is to live radically open, trusting radically, able to enjoy life with such passion that harming others is unthinkable. Strangely, we are deeply drawn to faith, while very scared of the life of faith. The life of faith is a life of love, trust, and openness, and it gives one free license to do whatever one wants. What scares us is that we are so used to laws and beliefs keeping our baser desires in check—for none of us lives constantly by faith—the prospect of faith providing a boundary for goodness is almost unimaginable.

In fact, it is unimaginable until one is touched by grace. Grace is the love of God that pours through the open heart, the heart of faith.

Paul Tillich (1955) writes,

Do you know what it means to be struck by grace? I does not mean that God exists, or that Jesus is the Savior, or that the Bible contains the truth. To believe that something is, is almost contrary to the meaning of grace. Furthermore, grace does not mean simply that we are making progress in our moral self-control, in our fight against special faults, and in our relationships to men and to society. Moral progress may be fruit of grace; but it is not grace itself, and it can even prevent us from receiving grace. For there is too often a graceless acceptance of Christian doctrines and a graceless battle against the structures of evil in our personalities. Such a graceless relation to God may lead us by necessity either to arrogance or to despair. It would be better to refuse God and the Christ and the Bible than to accept Them without grace. For if we accept without grace, we do so in the state of separation, and can only succeed in deepening the separation. We cannot transform our lives, unless we allow them to be transformed by that stroke of grace. It happens; or it does not happen. And certainly it does not happen if we try to force it upon ourselves, just as it shall not happen so long as we think, in our self-complacency, that we have no need of it. Grace strikes us when we are in great pain and restlessness. It strikes us when we walk through the dark valley of a meaningless and empty life. It strikes us when our disgust for our own being, our indifference, our weakness, our hostility, and our lack of direction and composure have become intolerable to us. It strikes us when, year after year, the longed-for perfection of life does not appear, when the old compulsions reign within us as they have for decades, when despair destroys all joy and courage. Sometimes at that moment a wave of light breaks into our darkness, and it is as though a voice were saying: "You are accepted. You are accepted, accepted by that which is greater than you, and the name of which you do not know. Do not ask for the name now; perhaps later you will do much. Do not seek for anything; do not perform anything; do not intend anything. Simply accept the fact that you are accepted!" If that happens to us, we experience grace. After such an experience we may not be better than before, and we may not believe more than before. But everything is transformed. In that moment, grace conquers sin, and reconciliation bridges the gulf of estrangement. And nothing is demanded of this experience, no religious or moral or intellectual presupposition, nothing but acceptance.

The second change that happens to clients in the therapeutic process is the discovery of the possibility of the life of faith. Those I interviewed told me over and over that they were warmed by the therapist's affirmation that it is worth looking into the matter of conflict more deeply. In other words, the therapist reinforced the validity of faith as a way to solve problems and seek happiness.

One of the great strengths of therapy is the invitation to openness, which is an invitation to faith—not to a system of beliefs, but to faith that is radically, trustfully open. Through this radical experience of openness flows the grace that Tillich writes so poignantly about. Through this faith, grace transforms everything.

CHAPTER SIXTEEN
DIFFERENTIATION OF SELF

Edwin Friedman, author of *Generation to Generation* (1984), writes that the central strengthening experience in a person's life is to become a "differentiated self." By this he means a person who has learned to live without differing to the expectations and pressures of family and culture first. The differentiated person is one who is able to ask first what feels right and second what might be seen as prudent among family and culture. In many ways Friedman's idealization of the differentiated person has its literary origin in Socrates affirmation of the self as well as in Henry David Thoreau's "Essay on Civil Disobedience." Thoreau argues that the free, happy person is one who first follows conscience, not the dictates of law and culture. The differentiated self, however, is more than just a free-spirited person. It is rooted in the knowledge of self, the deep awareness of one's inner processes and the ability to discern the meaning of one's surprising urgings and desires. By using the word "self" it resonates with Jungian psychology and its emphasis on the "individuated self."

I have learned to think of all therapy as systems therapy. A system is simply a unit of organization. Individuals are part of family systems, works systems, neighborhood systems, national systems, world system, eco-systems, etc. Systems thinking recognizes that all systems, large and small, operate out of some clear, definable rules and principles. The way I think about the systems client's live in is right out of the Bowen-Friedman school of thought.

In systems thinking we have learned an amazing fact: the level of seriousness in a system of relationships (a family, a work environment, a community, a government) is a barometer of the level of anxiety in that system. Families that are highly anxious are highly serious. Anxiety and playfulness simply do not mix. Whenever you see a family anxious over the behavior of a child, a probable marital squabble, and injured or ailing grandparent, you will see a high level of seriousness. Family members will tiptoe around any hint of the re-emergence of the problem, speaking glumly or often whispering as if they are holding a fragile vase. Because of this phenomena a family therapist immediately thinks, upon seeing such carefulness, that this is a problem with chronic anxiety.

Chronic anxiety is the greatest emotional roadblock to an individual's self-fulfillment. People in anxious families have their personal growth stunted. Anxiety is not an enjoyable emotion. So families with much anxiety seek ways to make the anxiety less uncomfortable. Their primary solution to reducing anxiety is predictability and familiarity, which serves the function of causing anxiety to be hidden, or unconscious. One of the most striking characteristics of families with chronic anxiety is the predictability of what will accompany certain behaviors. One of the most instructive questions a family therapist asks an anxious family is "What happens when . . . ?" Everyone can say exactly when each family member will do in response to a certain situation: "Joey will go outside; Jim will huff around the house griping about everything; Jane will go into the kitchen and cook and cry; June will whine about and complain that she's hungry." Anxious families learn to function in certain ways, in a systemic style, with each member playing certain roles and receiving certain attributes. Thus, a person's identity is defined by the family dynamics rather than oneself. Persons from unconsciously anxious families become undifferentiated people, enmeshed in family roles, expectations and attributes. Anxious families suffer from inflexibility, and their members are not free to be spontaneous and adventuresome.

All families experience many crises over the years. In the unconsciously anxious family, because their attempt to reduce anxiety is confined to roles and expectations (not consciously, though), there is a very small repertoire of responses to each crisis. When we have only a few optional responses to a crisis, the crisis is dangerous. With many options a crisis is an opportunity for change and growth.

When this pattern becomes intolerable to a family member or members because of marital problems, parenting problems, or illness, the priority focus for changing it must be on the anxiety so that self-definition may have substance.

The way to change a family or relationship system is simple: assume and maintain a non-reactive position that is different from what is expected. This is called a differentiated stance. Taking the stance might be easy, but maintaining it can be very difficult, for the family will predictably respond in two ways. First, it will attempt to seduce the person away from the new position, and if that doesn't work, it will, secondly attempt to sabotage the stance. Usually the method of choice is triangulation—getting three people involved in two people's problems, which effectively confuses issues and problems. Sometimes triangulation isn't between three people, but two people and a third issue that serves the same function as a third person. For example, one woman who finally took a firm position with her domineering father had to endure being blamed him for his stress-induced illness. Such serious methods of sabotage are what make sustaining change difficult. It's easy to change a family temporarily. It's very difficult to sustain that change. But . . . when such an attempt at sabotage is foiled, the family will respond by each member being confronted with their own feelings and the family will adjust to the change.

Families that are dysfunctional, which all are from time to time (Friedman says at least 20% of the time), usually they think that they are alienated from one another "big-time." Alienation, however is but a symptom of the trouble. Dysfunctional systems are in fact too close, or enmeshed. The most common word in dysfunctional families is "you." In dysfunctional systems the most common words are "us against them." Dysfunctional families "you" each other to death: "You bother me;" "You're doing it again;" "Why do you have to do that?" The antidote to "you" is "I". When a person takes a non-reactive "I" position, the whole system is caught by surprise. Immediately the family breaths a temporary sigh of relief. For a moment the fighting stops. Then the anxiety rises back up and seduction and sabotage set in. If the leader (the one who has dared to stand apart from the "you's") is able to maintain this new position, the family will do one of two things. Rarely, but sometimes, the leader gets shunned, cut off from the family. Mostly, though, individuals stand up and add their "I" to the dynamics. The leader finds allies. They, too, will have to withstand seduction and sabotage, but because someone else has cleared the way, it's usually not so difficult. And the whole family changes.

For example, a woman who had been consistently self-effacing and submissive to her husband's desires and point of view grew more and more angry. Having a poor sense of herself—for her views revolved so completely around her husband—she became critical and tacitly rebellious of him in order to push herself away from what felt like a smothering relationship. He responded with confusion, manipulation, and coercion. She became depressed, came into counseling, and came to realize that her desire to get further education for herself and claim some space was not really the problem. The problem was the undifferentiated relationship—emmeshment. She could work on that by simply being herself without apologies or secretiveness.

She announced to her husband her plans to go back to school, apologized to him for her secretiveness and fears of building a life of her own without his help, and added that after much reflection she had decided that her heretofore desires and efforts to be more self-sufficient were worth sharing openly with him. He responded silently, but his ensuing behavior led her to believe that he did not trust her resolve to actually be different with him. His expectations of her increased, his annoyance with her escalated, and tension at home mounted. She, however, felt better than ever, wondering aloud why she had abandoned her early adult self-confidence for dependency and its related depression. In spite of occasional backsliding, she maintained her new stance with gradually diminishing anxiety.

He, in turn, paid a few visits to his pastor, who asked him at one point if he was strong enough to take his wife's changes. He decided he was, cut down on his exhaustive work schedule, got to know his children better, and eventually the marriage regained its peace, this time with a relationship accepting of change and differences.

They had developed a relationship between two differentiated people rather than between co-dependents (two people leaning on one another to protect themselves from life's problems). As they learned to stand apart from one another, they learned to focus on the real other person, not the imagined partner, and their strength to face life less anxiously increased.

Anxiety always threatens to be a disabling emotion. One need only sit for a few minutes with a person suffering from overwhelming anxiety or a panic attack before the sympathetic feeling of complete loss of self and freedom arises. Experiencing waves of anxiety is horrible. It is an experience of being totally without defense, as if one's skin has been striped from the body. It is a boundary-less state, one in which the anxiety-riddled individual has no sense of substantial self, only a horrible feeling of being "at the mercy of". It is a thoroughly undifferentiated state. Certainly medicines are needed to treat endogenous anxiety, but the psycho-social answer to high anxiety is the differentiation process.

Differentiation is becoming a self separate from others. It is a boundary-making process, an empowering process. It enables one to have choices, to make decisions, to be different from others as well as to freely join with them. Differentiation gives one the capacity to affirm the paradox of connectedness and separateness (that we are fundamentally connected and fundamentally separated from one another). Without such affirmation faith is too shallow to be really life-transforming, for the undifferentiated self is drowning in unrelenting anxiety. Without differentiation, our vision is short-sighted because the Inner Light is dimmed by chronic anxiety.

However, there is a difference between existential anxiety and pathological chronic anxiety. The types of existential anxiety Paul Tillich (1952) names, the anxiety of doubt and meaninglessness, the anxiety of death and finitude, and the anxiety of guilt and condemnation, are normal even for the differentiated and healthy person. These are experiences that are indelible parts of life. Because we are finite we will experience periods of anxiety over our fate and pending death. Because there is no absolute answer to the reason for our existence—there is no answer that cannot be questioned—we will struggle with doubts and questions about our meaningfulness. Because we are always aware of the imperfection of our efforts as well as our secret thoughts and desires, we will struggle with guilt and wonder about ultimate judgment. The healthy person is one who can face existential anxiety and be happy *in spite of* it. To be able to have the courage to say "Yes" to life while acknowledging life's unanswerable questions, living with the great unknowns, is at the essence of fullness and happiness—in spite of nagging anxiety.

Families mired in chronic anxiety are composed of persons who do not have the courage to accept existential anxiety, and therefore they work at burying it. But since emotions are indigestible, the anxiety becomes like a bleeding ulcer that is sinister and disabling. The fact is that the most unconsciously anxious families are the ones that are working the hardest to avoid anxiety. We cannot avoid anxiety; however, we can transcend its disabling power by accepting it and living fully in spite of its occasional sting.

There are three common pseudo-solutions to existential anxiety which are solutions characteristic of chronically anxious systems. First there is the attempt to control through compulsive behavior and demands. There are thousands of examples of this being the style of chronically anxious work systems. In an atmosphere of chronic anxiety, someone or a group attempts to manage the negativity by making rigid rules and standards. They take an axe to anything nonconforming. Things get done, but fingers get chopped off. The price for compulsivity is a heaviness, and over-riding seriousness. There is little fun.

The second pseudo-solution is addiction. Addictive people attempt to bend their minds away from anxiety. Drugs and alcohol are obvious in how they bend minds and make us feel "better" or ignorant of the problems, but addiction can also appear benign. Television is very addictive, as are computer games and the internet, junk novels, watching sports. Anything habit-forming can become mildly addictive. These mild addictive habits spiral us down slowly, unlike major addictions like chemical addictions, binge eating, gambling, and sexual addictions. Major addictions lead us fairly quickly to jail or death. Minor addictions destroy us slowly. The price we pay for addictions, mild and major, is a shallow spirituality and a lack of intimacy. I believe that the purpose of an addiction is to avoid intimacy, for intimacy always holds us closer to our own personal pain, which the addict is loath to confront. Spirituality, which is based on openness, is also thwarted by addictions, for an addiction is meant to close our eyes and bend our attention away from what we feel and need. Spirituality is about focusing on our greatest needs and most powerful feelings. Addiction dulls our spiritual quest.

The third pseudo-solution is obsession or delusion. In obsessive systems people focus on imaginary problems in order to divert themselves from the real issues. They work at keeping up with the Jones or their competitors at a pace and intensity level that keep them off of themselves. They have a tendency to be paranoid, wondering who is out to get them or what bad will happen next. They are big on Murphy's Law and are chronic worriers. They also are hard to pin down. They often have a histrionic style that jumps from issue to issue so quickly that few tasks are satisfactorily completed. Obsession systems often are spread too thin, doing much too much to be of high quality in anything. The price for obsessiveness is a terrible lack of effectiveness. To stay obsessed robs one of effective discipline. People who are obsessively oriented are rarely very competent and therefore rarely very confident.

Delusions happen when obsessiveness becomes extreme. A delusion is an obsessive thought based on an anxious interpretation of some simple fact. Instead of grasping the real importance of the fact, the deluded person interprets the fact subjectively and unrealistically. Delusion is actually the logical consequence of obsessiveness. For example, a person obsessed with fears of black persons might, upon hearing news reports on a few particular criminals, develop a delusional prejudice that allows no exceptions to the view that all black persons are dangerous. The obsession with race, which is disabling enough, becomes a delusion that thoroughly alienates the person from healthy relations with black persons.

These three pseudo-solutions to chronic anxiety are always connected. They cannot exist without the others, but they are seen in degrees of style. An addictive person feels compelled to do what he or she is addicted to, and will become obsessed with thoughts of how to maintain the addiction without it causing other problems. An obsessive person will compulsively perform task after task, but be easily distracted as if addicted to change or crisis or out-rage. The compulsive person will be hung up on details to the point of neither seeing nor thinking of anything else, as if addicted to an idea. Regardless of the degree of focus, all three pseudo-solutions are reactions to the problem of anxiety. They seek to manage chronic anxiety in order to keep existential anxiety underground.

The systemic solution to these pseudo-solutions is to confront compulsion with playfulness (for compulsion is far too serious), addiction with spirituality (which is what we have learned best from Alcoholics Anonymous), and obsession with discipline.

For example, when working with a compulsive client, I often joke, banter, and satirize. I might tell compulsives who are asking me what they should do to get a lobotomy. Said at the right time, such playfulness is funny and disarms the compulsive defense, even if only temporarily. I sometimes think that the worse treatment for a compulsive is being too professional or too careful. The movie character Colombo is a model for working with compulsive clients. Keep 'em off balance so they can't figure out what to do.

Alcoholics Anonymous and its sister organizations have the spiritual alternative to addictions down to a science in the "Twelve Steps" programs. It confronts addictive behavior not only with a focus on the real problem, but also gives the participant an alternative spiritual discipline that offers healing and health instead of chaos and stress. I refer most of my addictive clients to the Twelve Step model. The ones who are turned off to Twelve Steps I encourage them to be open to the spiritual discipline it offers, even if they won't step into an A.A. meeting.

Obsessive people often come across highly spiritual, but there is a shallowness to it because of the lack of discipline and focus. Obsessiveness must be met with discipline, and at root discipline requires the ability to step back and focus more clearly. Obsessive people are usually too close to the issue to see it clearly. Just as if you hold your hand right up to your nose and then can't focus on it, obsessive people see problems out of focus because they are too enmeshed with them. What they must learn is to pull back, to differentiate. Differentiation provides enough distance to allow good focus, so that discipline can be effective and productive.

The differentiation process is focused on learning to live comfortably with anxiety and problems. To do so allows one to be productive and creative. And productivity and creativity is tied to faith, for faith opens us up to possibilities and potentials even while anxiety threatens to close us down. In this process we move from faith to life more abundant. Tillich (1952) calls this "the state of being grasped by the God beyond God." Despite the fact that we come finally to the realization that there are no ultimate answers that fully satisfy us, just at that moment, we experience a sense of God that transcends the god we had set up for ourselves.

Anxiety always tempts us to ground ourselves in pseudo-solutions like materialism, religious fundamentalism, totalitarianism, or creating a god that has no transcendence. Choosing such a life is an attempt to find security by eliminating anxiety, by turning our backs on questions and doubts. It is a solution that relies on externals. By making a book, a person, a philosophy, or a group wholly sacred and unquestionable—dogmatic—existential anxiety might be avoided, but with it goes the potential for wisdom that accompanies the courage to live in spite of anxiety. Such idol worship sets up chronic anxiety. There is a heavy price for fundamentalism, materialism, totalitarianism, and non-transcendent religion. By immersing oneself in such controlling and defensive world-views, the openness necessary for the discovery of the Inner Light is lost. There can be no "God within" when God is defined from without.

The good thing for the therapist is that when a client comes to me who is caught up in such pseudo-solutions, he or she is admitting on some level that it is actually a "solution" that doesn't work. My job is to align myself with that part of the client that is questioning the validity of the old response. In doing so I am an ally to the forces for self-actualization and courage and an enemy to the god that is too small.

Differentiation is to faith what anxiety is to life. By denying anxiety through pseudo-solutions to doubt, questions about our fate, meaninglessness, and guilt, we deny ourselves a full life. Life is full and rich when we have the courage to live in spite of existential anxiety. This is at root a differentiated stance. And faith is insubstantial without the freedom and strength inherent in differentiation.

The differentiation process also gives one the capacity to love. Just as we let ourselves be, we are able to let-be. We cannot love someone when we are too close to focus and see, when we are too undifferentiated. Instead, we simply "need" that person. Such enmeshment is disabling, not enabling. We love by letting-be in an enabling sense. Learning to love is the first step in the process of the realization of the Inner Light as guide in one's life.

CHAPTER SEVENTEEN
DEEPENING OF SOUL

As a person develops a sense of humbleness, the openness of faith and subsequent experience of grace, and the confidence of self-differentiation, there is a deepening of the soul, an experience of being drawn to the Inner Light of God. This is the spiritual awakening that began in infancy but reaches its full fruition in adulthood. It is the fourth great transformation in the psychotherapeutic process.

Spirituality is awakened in four phases: experiencing and building relationships, experiencing physical actualization, unity of body and mind, and wrestling with decline, generativity, and dying.

First is the primacy of relationships. This begins in childhood with the bonding and development of relationships within the family. It gains momentum in adolescence with the advent of choice in intimacy, i.e., picking one's own friends and lovers instead of them being chosen by parents and relatives. With marriage or the intimate friendships of the young adult years, relationships become a bridge to meaning and self-fulfillment.

Second is physically-based spirituality. The young adult, male and female, is fascinated and moved by physical ability. The more disciplined the young adult is physically, the more deeply he/she will experience the moving of the Spirit in the physical world. It is simply awesome what the young body can do. A physically fit young man has amazing stamina, terrific balance, incredible power, and wonderful ability to recover from hurt and fatigue. A young woman, likewise, has great endurance and recovery from stress, as well as the special ability to carry and give birth to another human being. For those who choose to blossom physically by keeping physically fit, there is a deep affirmation of the life of the spirit.

As the adult matures and the body declines in ability, one must come to terms with the unity of the body and mind. Aging brings about two physical realizations: the inability to keep up with the stamina and power of those younger, and muscular control beyond the ability of youth. How often the older man will comment, "If only I had the body control then, when I was so strong, that I do now!" It's not just physical control, though. There is a sense of control that comes with wisdom and experience. The mature adult can take life more in stride, for he/she isn't so surprised by problems. Anxiety is not so overwhelming and relaxation and peacefulness rise.

As one continues to age, anxiety over death cannot help but intensify. This fourth stage of development is the confrontation with that reality and the necessity to find a way to transcend death itself. People do so best by noticing and affirming the cycle of life and its perpetuation through our generativity. In other words, we find meaning in passing along wisdom and creations. The grandparent's task is to pass along the torch, affirming the contribution inherent in the success of the next generation. It is simply the affirmation that I have touched the world just as it has blessed me with its richness of experience.

In a way, life at its essence is quite simple. It is experience, some intense, some gentle. To be able to affirm life is to embrace all of its experiences, finding the wisdom and blessing in them all. This is hard to do, of course, when experiences include such tragedies as the death of a child, but I've come to understand that even tragedy connects us to others in healing ways. When a person who has experienced the death of a child meets another who has just suffered such a tragedy, the possibility of comforting that survivor is deepened immensely. There is a connection that only the richness of life can offer. The Spirit moves in such circles. I have heard people who have suffered great tragedy remark, "I never would have thought that such suffering would have been my blessing; I never could have ministered to others had I not felt such pain." I am such a person. I know that I never would have been a pastoral counselor had I not had the horrible experience of suffering through an irreparable marriage and sought the wisdom to save it. That curse has become my blessing.

Life is a gift, all of it. Even what we cower from has implicitly in it a blessing to give. Wisdom is borne out of suffering, and wisdom lightens the load of our toil and connects us to those whom we can love.

It is my job to convey this simple claim, and it can be affirmed most fully at the spiritual level, the level where mystery is smiled at.

When I interviewed persons about their therapeutic experience, they all talked of a deepening process that pointed to an affirmation of a higher wisdom, an Inner Light, that was evident in dreams, prayer life, study of great spiritual texts, and a sort of spiritual intuition—revelation. Thus, I came to realize that the fourth great change in the psychotherapeutic process is the deepening of the soul, the newfound affirmation of the importance of communication with the Divine, receptiveness to the in-breaking of the Spirit. In theology we call this an *epiphania*, an in-breaking of light.

There is a story in I Samuel that is quite instructive on this matter.

In those days, when the boy Samuel was serving the Lord under the direction of Eli, there were very few messages from the Lord, and visions from him were quite rare. One night Eli, who was now almost blind, was sleeping in his own room; Samuel was sleeping in a sanctuary, where the sacred Covenant Box was. Before dawn, while the lamp was still burning, the Lord called Samuel, He answered, "Yes, sir?" and ran to Eli and said, "You called me, and here I am."

But Eli answered, "I didn't call you; go back to bed." So Samuel went back to bed.

The Lord called Samuel again. The boy did not know that it was the Lord, because the Lord had never spoken to him before. So he got up, went to Eli, and said, "You called me, and here I am."

But Eli answered, "My son, I didn't call you; go back to bed."

The Lord called Samuel a third time; he got up, went to Eli, and said, "You called me, and here I am."

Then Eli realized that it was the Lord who was calling the boy, so he said to him, "Go back to bed; and if he calls you again, say, 'Speak, Lord, your servant is listening.'" So Samuel went back to bed.

The Lord came and stood there, and called as he had before, "Samuel! Samuel!"

Samuel answered, "Speak; your servant is listening." (I Samuel 3:1-10, *Today's English Version*)

At that point, God instructed Samuel on his role as a prophet, which began a major transformation in Israelite history: the Davidic monarchy.

This story illustrates the deepening of soul which so radically changes people. People in therapy typically have an awakening, a call, that they at first don't understand, don't trust, and don't believe. Usually the therapist is just like Eli, too, not fully aware of the significance of this in-breaking of light, and sort of tells the client to go back to bed, or worse, suggests medication to fight off psychosis, mixing up spiritual matters with psychological delusions. But the call keeps breaking in, until even the most dense therapist senses its significance and suggests that the client pay attention. Those who do pay attention find a rich, deep source of wisdom and direction that is liberating.

CHAPTER EIGHTEEN
CONCLUSION

In this book I have sought to provide the reader with a description of a craft, a primer for doing psychotherapy. I've also sought to present the unique perspective of the pastoral counselor, which includes a theological foundation not necessarily inherent in the training and perspective of the secularly trained psychotherapist. It is this perspective which makes the theoretical foundation of this book apply to much more than just this one craft. Psychotherapy, thus, becomes a metaphor for any craft, any art, any science.

Christian theology's foundation is the study of the Bible. Biblical study has many complicated facts and interpretative tools, but in essence it is based upon a simple triangular study-guide: text, context, and you. The text, of course, is the Biblical passage or story. The context is the historical, social, religious, political, economic, and personal aspects of the writer and/or teller of that story. You, of course, is the reader's reaction. Biblical studies often have focused on the text and context and presumed the reader will find his/her own way. The better way, however, is to pay close attention to the reactions and projections of the reader, for the Bible was written to change people. All canonical literature (all the great religious texts) were not written for mere entertainment, but for transformation.

Psychotherapy is similar. It is not just an entertainment exercise. It's purpose is transformation or healing. The greatest intellectual contributions in the field of psychotherapy have been in the areas of "text"—studies of patients—and "you", i.e., essays meant to help the psychotherapist gain personal insight. This book is a contribution to "context". My concern here has been to illuminate the details of how to create a sanctuary for healing, transformative psychotherapy. I have done so with the knowledge that psychotherapy takes on all styles and formats. But I know that any style must take the details of the process seriously, just as I have. My own style as a pastoral counselor will be different, more or less, than someone else's. It has integrity, though, and, hopefully, will serve as a model for other therapists to find their own integrity and stay true to themselves.

I was a champion distance runner during my 20s. I did have talent, but my talent only presented me with possibilities some others didn't have. In deciding to seek to actualize that talent, I studied form and tried lots of innovative workouts. I paid close attention to details. I learned from running that success in any endeavor depends on motivation, attention to detail, and, to some degree, talent. Being a psychotherapist is no different.

I also learned from running that despite it being primarily a craft, at its highest levels it was an expressive art. When I ran my best I came to realize that I was expressing artistic beauty. I've yet to find any artistic endeavor that was any more expressive of beauty and form than what running became for me. I learned that any craft, when developed fully, turns into art. The transformation that takes place happens when the Spirit breaks into the activity. But this *epiphania* does not happen accidentally. It happens in the midst of intensive discipline.

There is no doubt in my mind that psychotherapy is first and foremost a craft that is taught and learned through attention to details and careful understanding of the patient, but the essence of psychotherapy does not stop with craftmanship. At some point in the development of the psychotherapeutic skill, God enters the sanctuary and the craft becomes a sacred art. It is at this point that psychotherapy becomes an expression of being, a creative process. That's where activities like running and psychotherapy meet: they are both, at their very best levels, re-creational.

Strangely enough, as I've completed this book, I've had trouble with its content. For months I sat on this discomfort, laying the manuscript aside. One day, though, I realized the reason for my discomfort. I'm bothered by the book's seriousness! Although I still pay serious attention to the details of the sanctuary for psychotherapy that I work out of, at a point in my development as a psychotherapist I have stopped being so serious about much of the work. Now I laugh a lot more with my patients. I joke with them, have fun. Now, for me, being a psychotherapist is more recreational. It's more fun than it used to be.

Running was the same way for me. For a long time running was mostly hard work—toil. Then one day—I still remember the day—I found myself "running free" (that's what I called it). It was joyful, and running was never the same. There were still "work days", but on the whole I could now train hard and have fun.

A psychotherapist must toil over the details of the therapeutic sanctuary. It is a necessary discipline, and there is no shortcut. At some point, though, the work itself will be transformed from craft to art, from work to recreation. This is the *epiphania* that we seek in all our disciplined endeavors. It will happen in some unexpected way, and we toil away with the confidence that it will happen. It is what gives meaning and clarity to the work.

So my advice is simple: create a therapeutic sanctuary that is as carefully designed as I have sought to convey in this book. Then stick with it and do careful work. It will not only enable you to be a good therapist, it might also give you a blessing that can only come from God.

BIBLIOGRAPHY

A.A.P.C. Directory. Fairfax, VA: AAPC, 1993.

Diagnostic and Statistic Manual, III, The American Psychiatric Association. Washington, D.C.: APA, 1980.

Easwaran, Eknath, "Information Age Trivializes Education, in *Truthseeker* (Newsletter of the M.K. Gandhi Institute for Nonviolence), (650 E. Parkway S, Memphis, TN 38104), Fall 1994, p. 5, reprinted from *Blue Mountain—A Journal for Spiritual Living*.

Kopp, Sheldon, *Back to One: A Practical Guide for Psychotherapists*. Palo Alto, CA: Science and Behavior Books, 1977.

"Newsletter" of the American Association of Pastoral Counselors. Fairfax, VA: Fall 1992.

Tillich, Paul, *The Shaking of the Foundations*. N.Y.: Charles Scribner's Sons, 1948.

Tillich, Paul, *The Courage to Be*. New Haven: Yale University Press, 1952.

ABOUT THE AUTHOR

Ron McDonald is a pastoral counselor with the Church Health Center, a not-for-profit health care clinic for the working poor of Memphis, Tennessee, where he also lives with his wife and two sons. He has been a pastoral counselor in various settings since 1979. He graduated from Hendrix College in Conway, Arkansas, in 1973, Union Theological Seminary in New York City in 1977, earning a Master of Divinity degree, and Saint Paul School of Theology in Kansas City, Missouri, in 1988, earning a Doctor of Ministry degree. He received his clinical training from the Training Institute for Counseling and Therapy of the Foundation for Religion and Mental Health in Briarcliff Manor, New York, graduating in 1983. He became a member of The American Association of Pastoral Counselors in 1984 and is now a Diplomate in that organization. He is a Quaker.

Additionally, he is a folksinger who performs with his guitar and hammer dulcimer and a storyteller.

Dr. McDonald's website is www.ron-mcdonald.com.

CPSIA information can be obtained at www.ICGtesting.com
Printed in the USA
LVOW122222011012

301047LV00001B/3/P